Visions of Beauty II

Images of 12 Figure Models

By Gary D. Melton

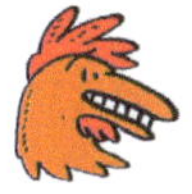

Goofy Rooster Publishing
Wylie, Texas
www.goofyrooster-publishing.com

Visions of Beauty II

Images of 12 Figure Models

By Gary D. Melton

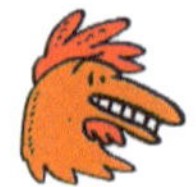

Goofy Rooster Publishing PO Box 2904 Wylie, Texas 75098
www.goofyrooster-publishing.com

ISBN-10: 0-9843940-5-2

ISBN-13: 978-0-9843940-5-0

Copyright © 2010 by Gary D. Melton

All photographs Copyright © 2010 by Gary D. Melton

All rights reserved. No part of this book may be reproduced or transmitted in any form or by any means, electronic or mechanical, including photocopying, recording or by any information storage and retrieval system, without written permission from the author, except for the inclusion of brief quotations in a review.

Table of Contents

Introduction

I created the original "Visions of Beauty" for myself. I had been photographing models for some time and wanted to put together some of my best work in a book. Now, almost two years later - I decided to create a sequel to it - and make it available to a wider audience.

The original book included photos of 12 figure models - six of which are included in this book as well: Carlotta, Isobel, Jeska, Katy, Liz and London. I've placed six of their best photos from the original book here (but I re-edited them all first). I've also included ten "new" photos of them that have never been published anywhere before.

Six models who weren't in the first book appear here in 18 additional photos: Amanda, Brittney, Jess, Jessica M, Jessica V and Nikki. [FYI: you can see more of Brittney, Jess and Jessica M in my book: "Nine Women Revealed: *Intimate Revelations of Nine Real Women in Images and Words*."]

I really appreciate the incredible beauty of the female form, which I continually strive to capture with my photos - I hope you enjoy the works I've created here in "Visions of Beauty II"!

Gary Melton

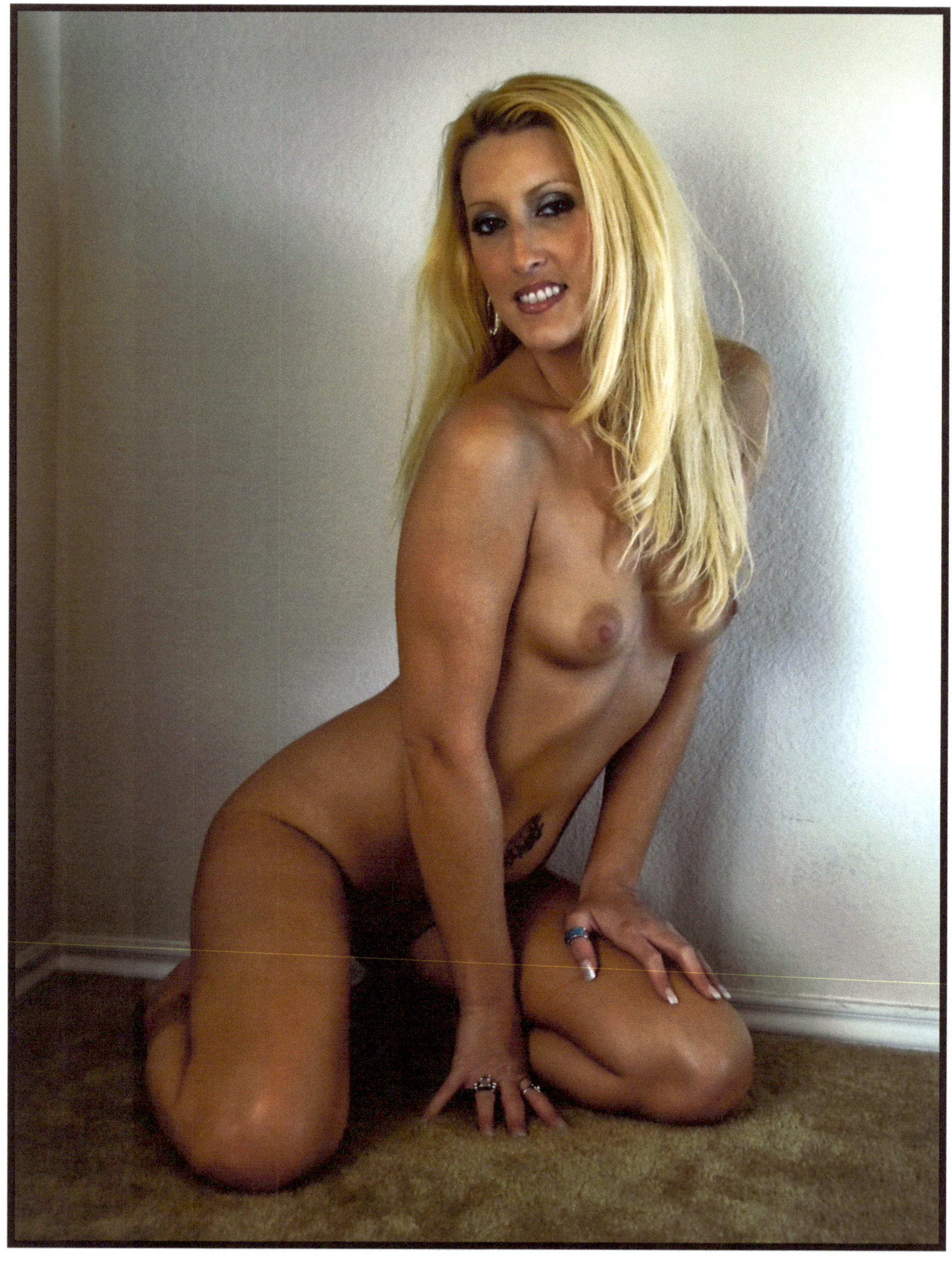

Amanda

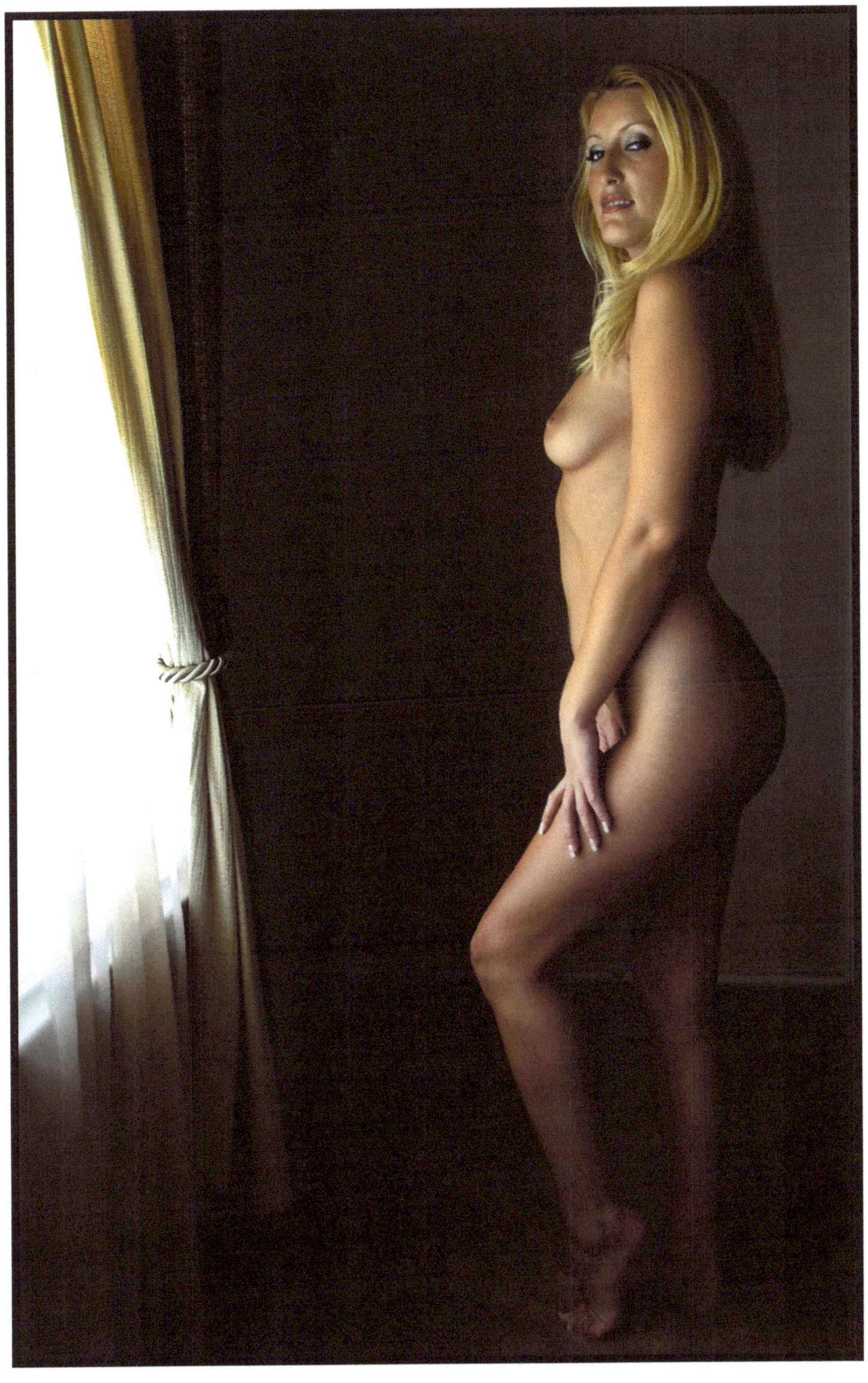

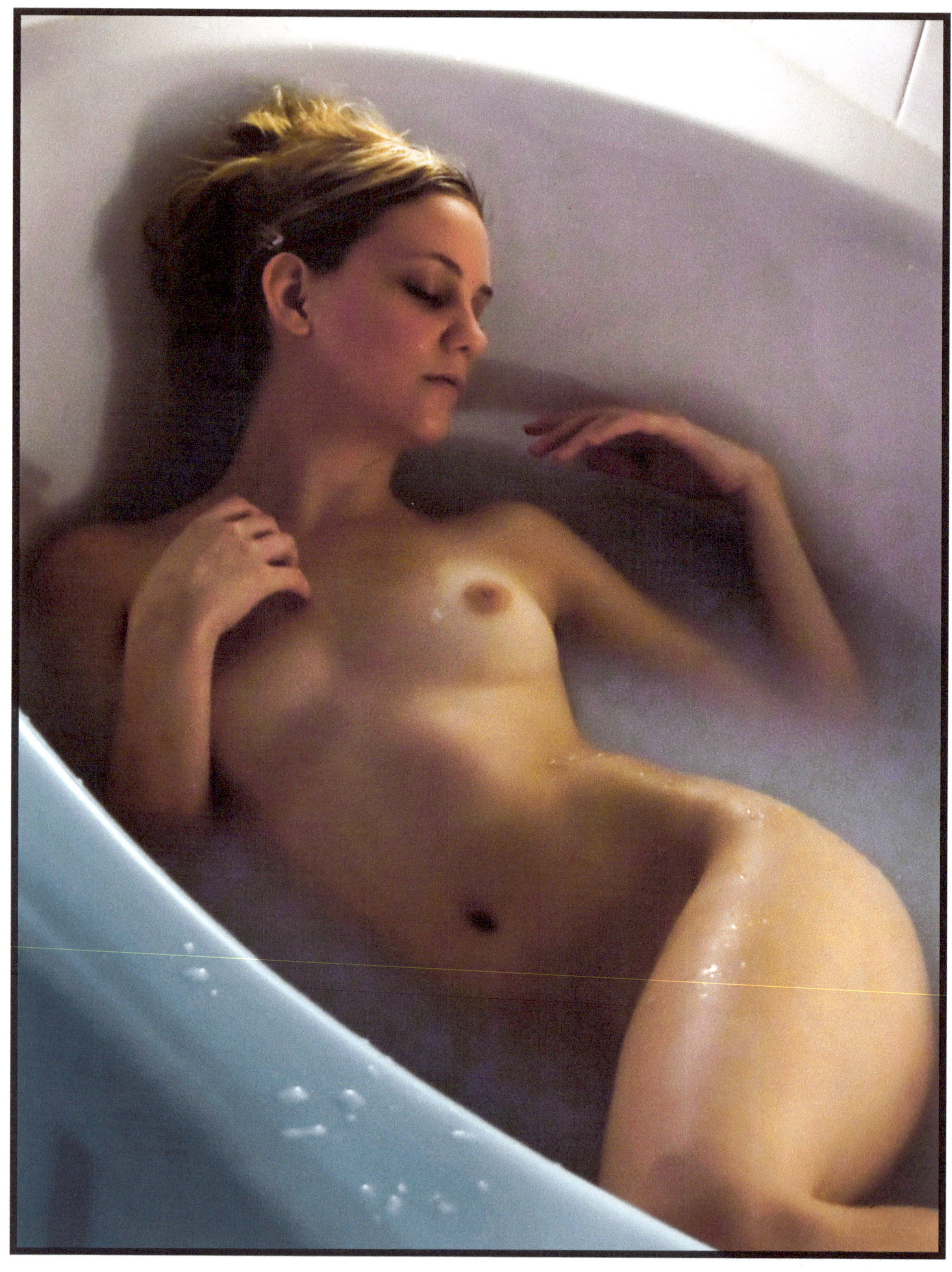

Brittney

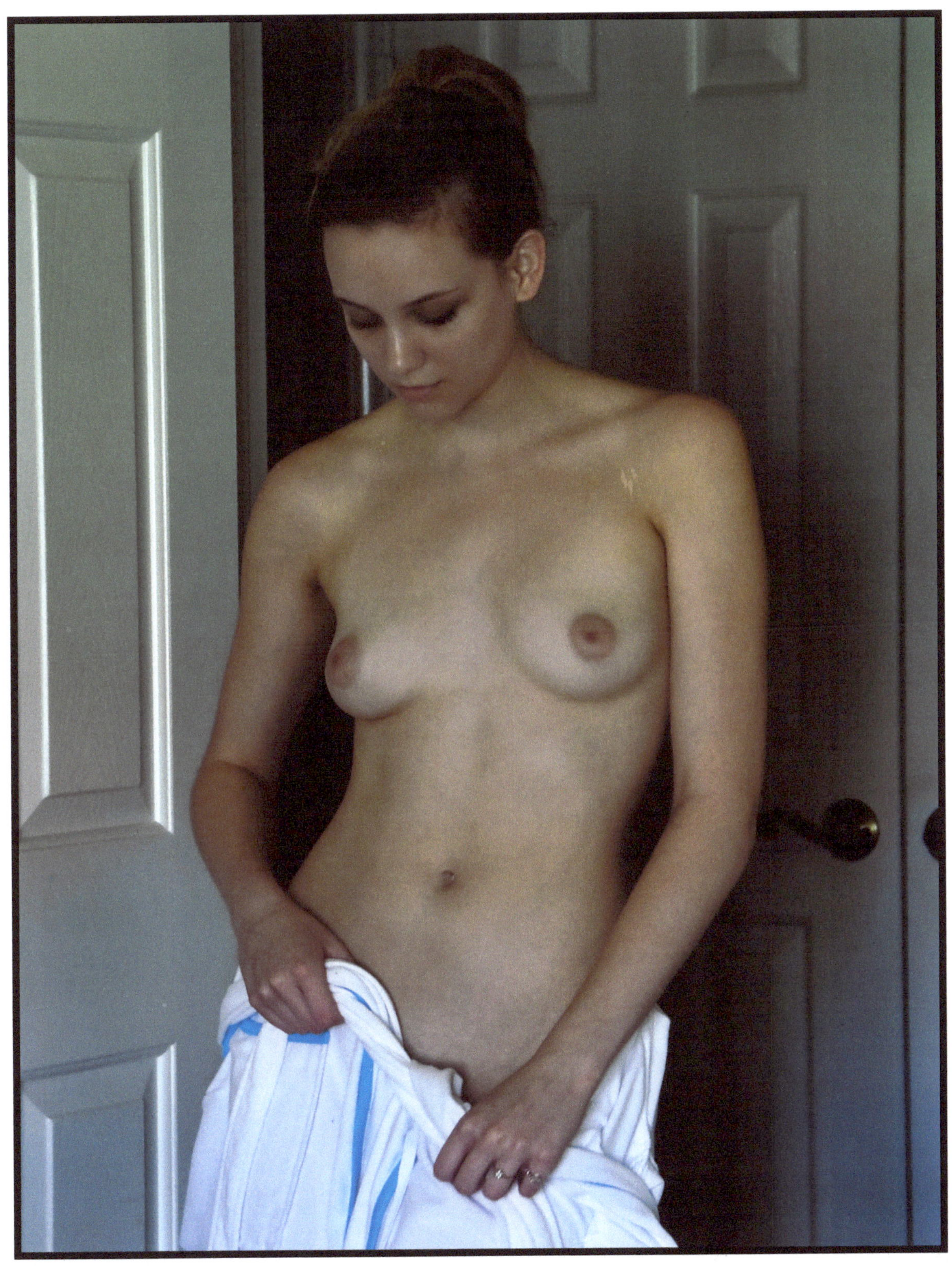

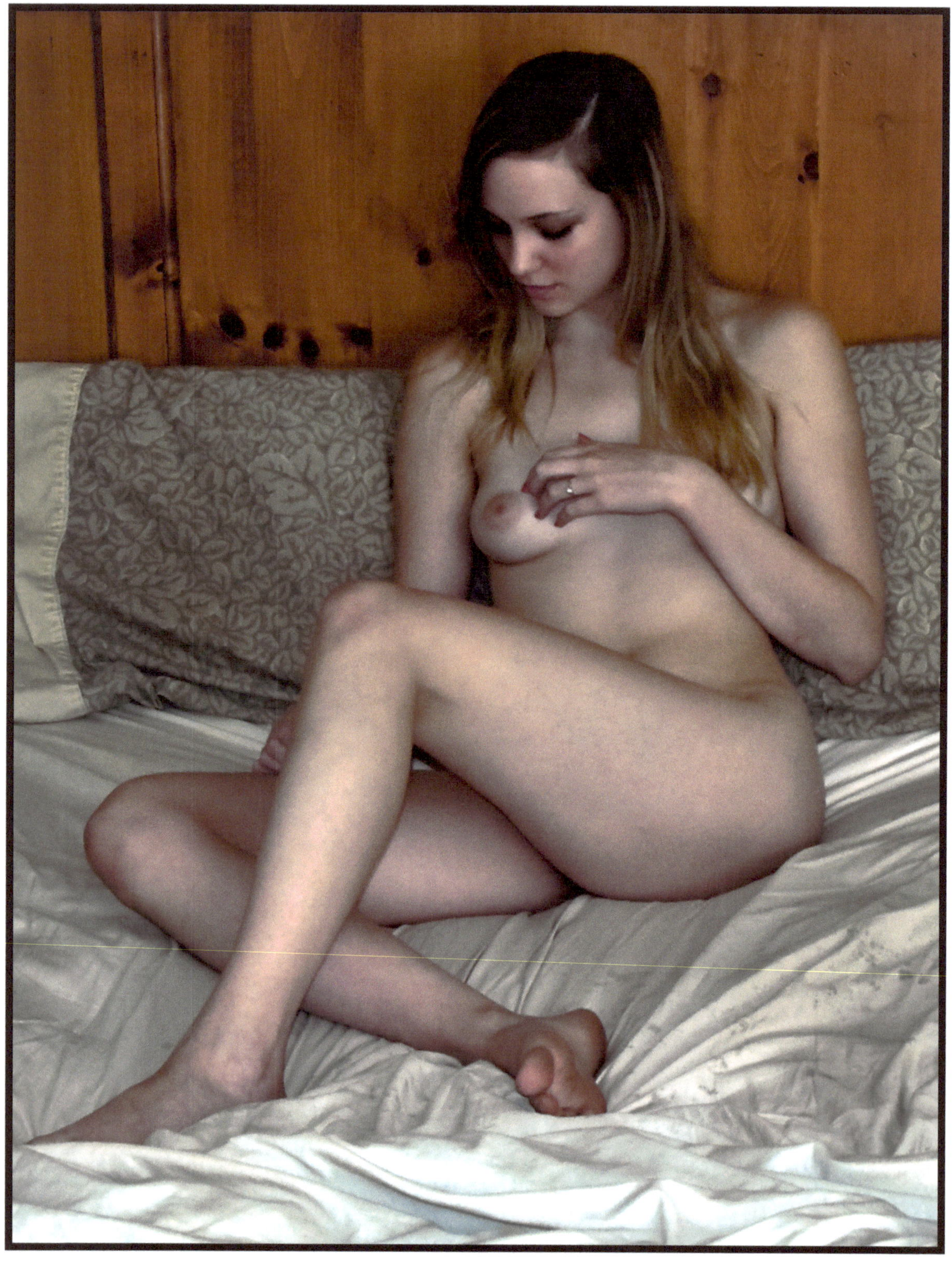

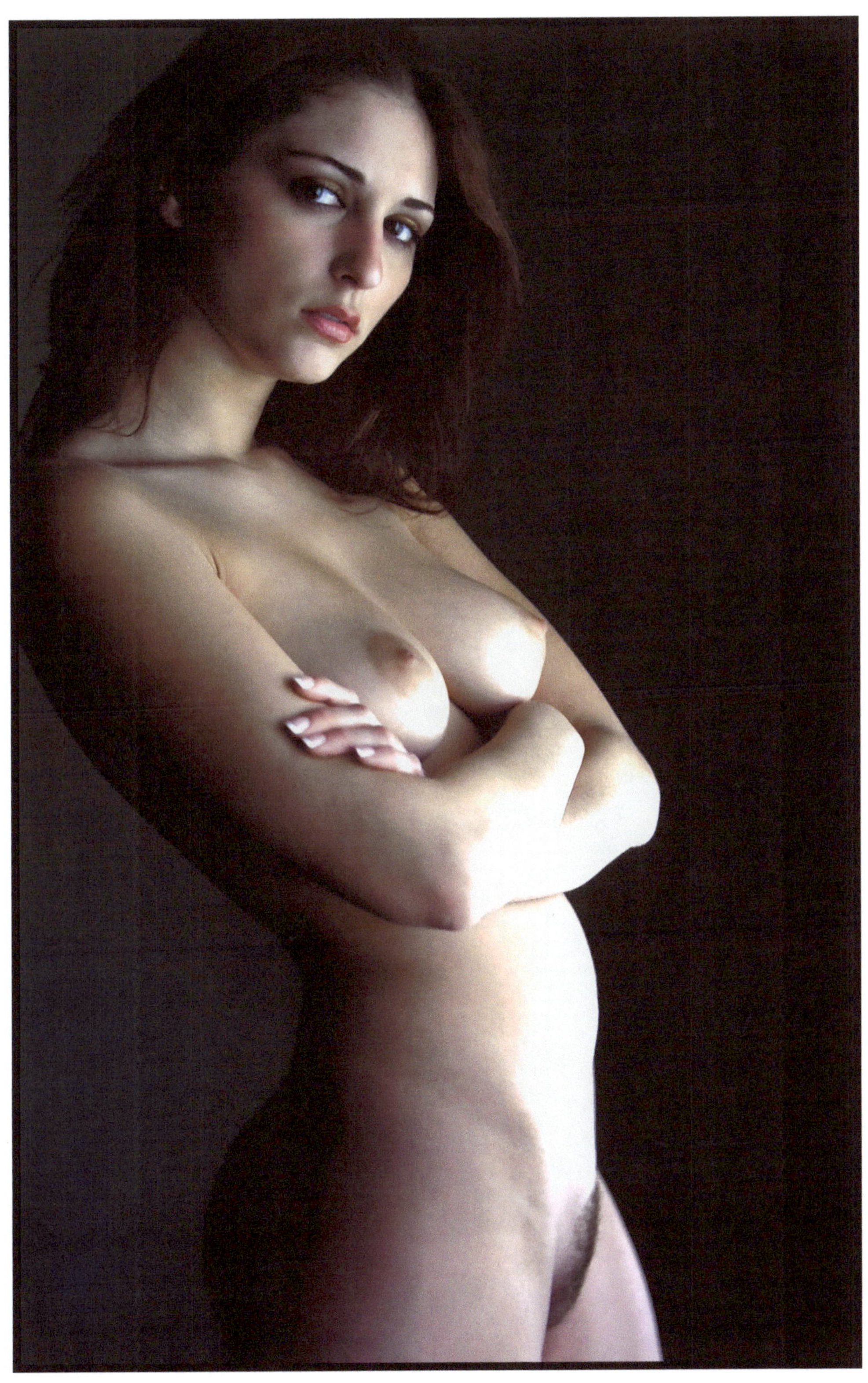

Carlotta

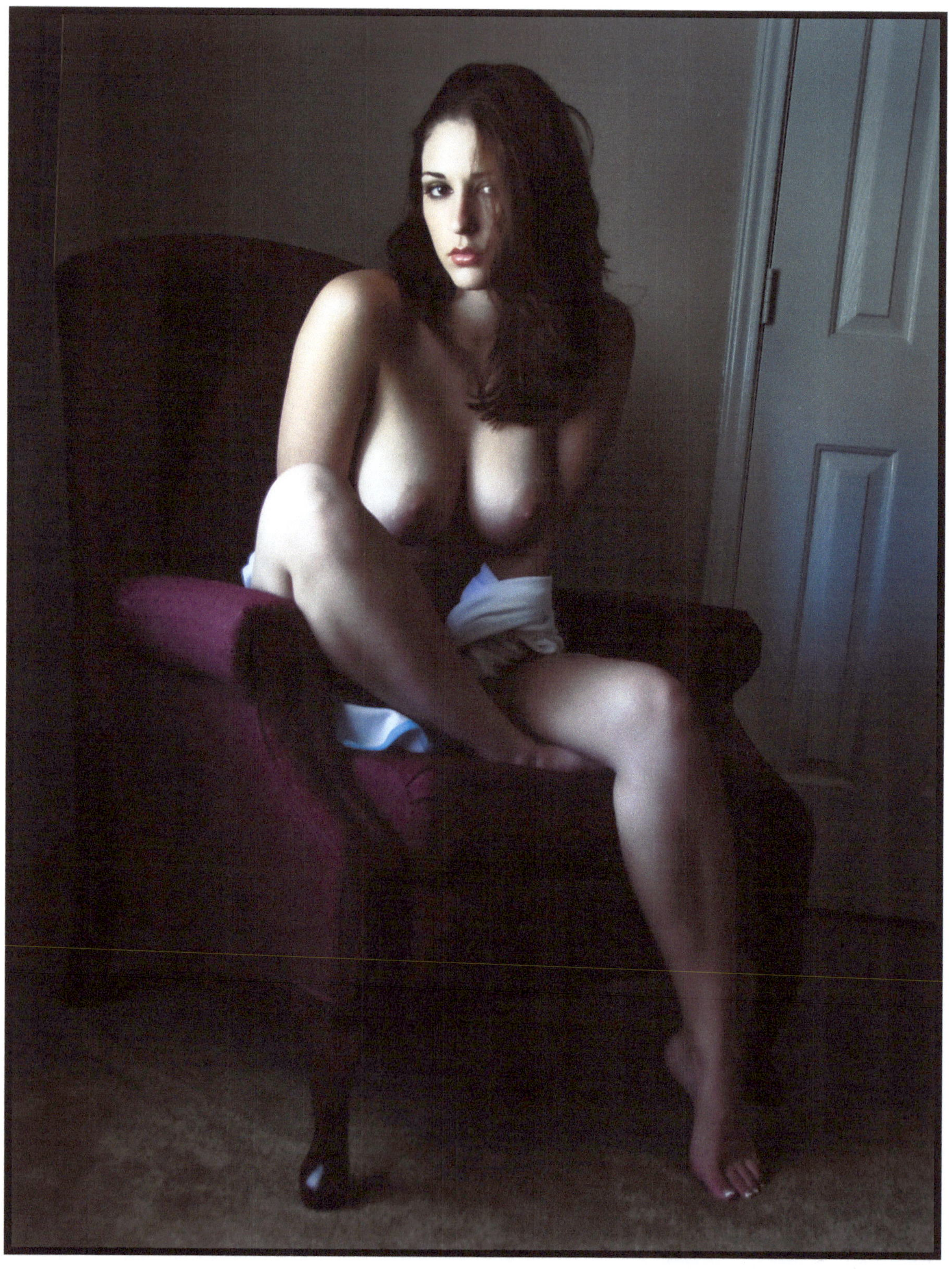

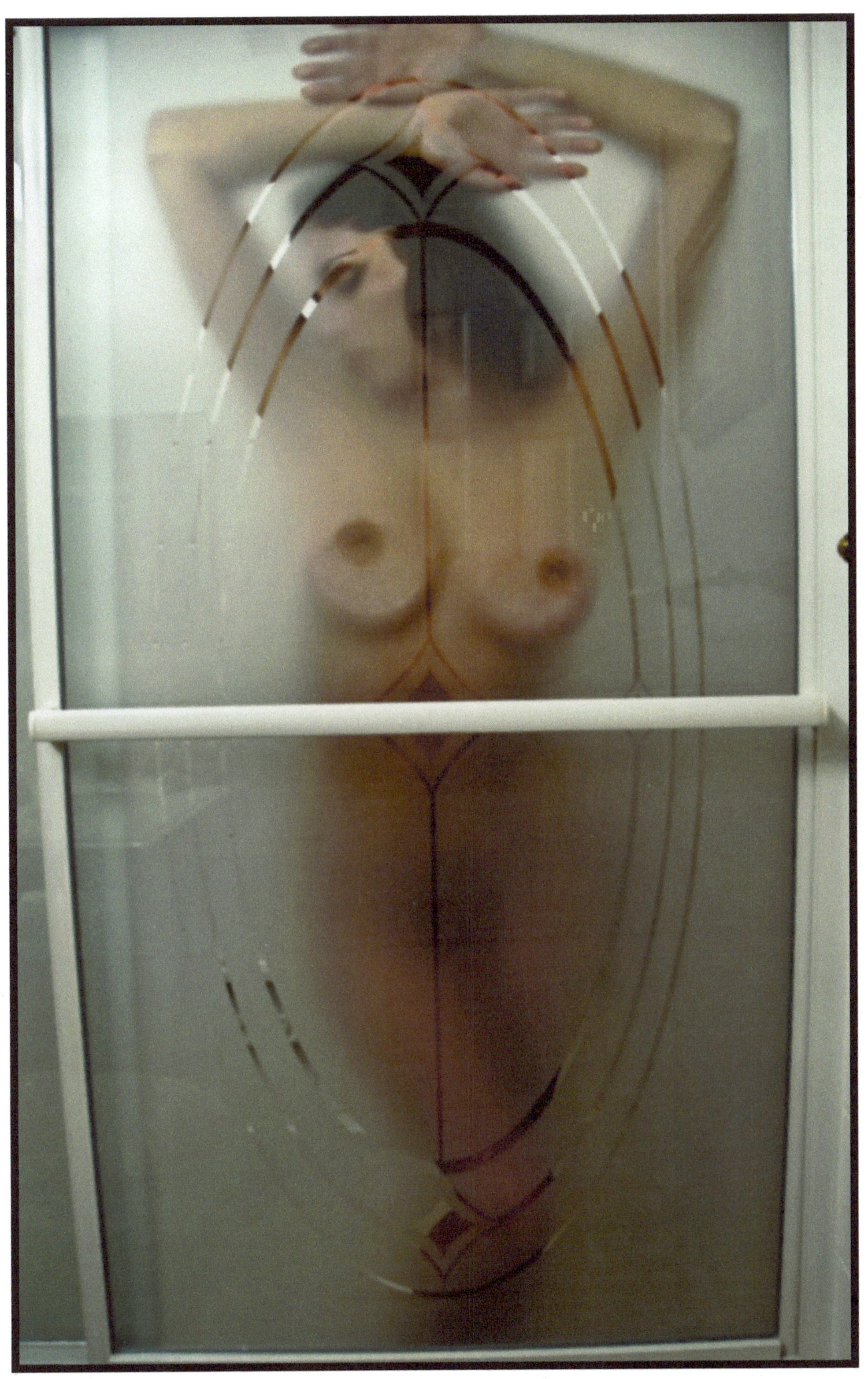

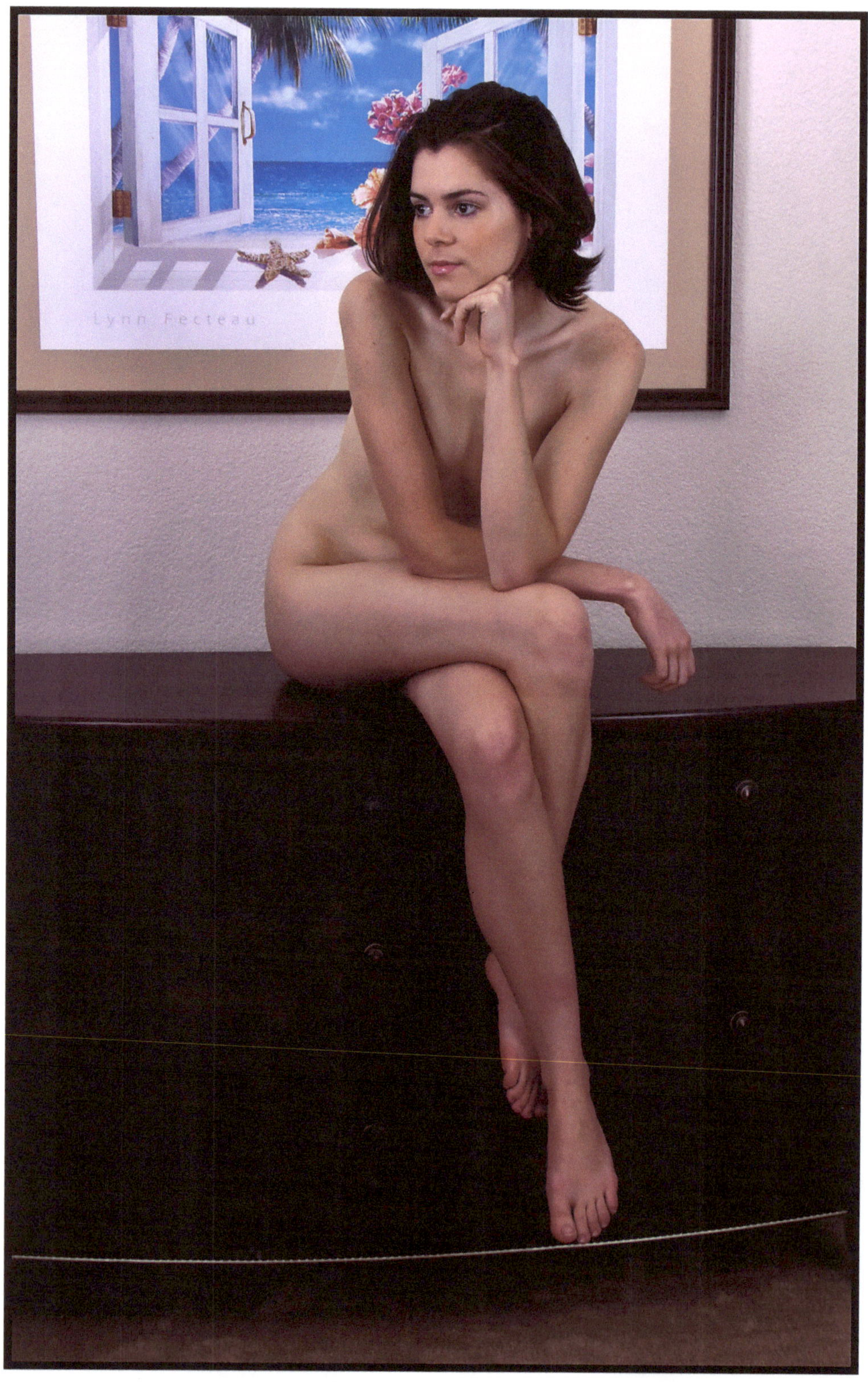

Isobel

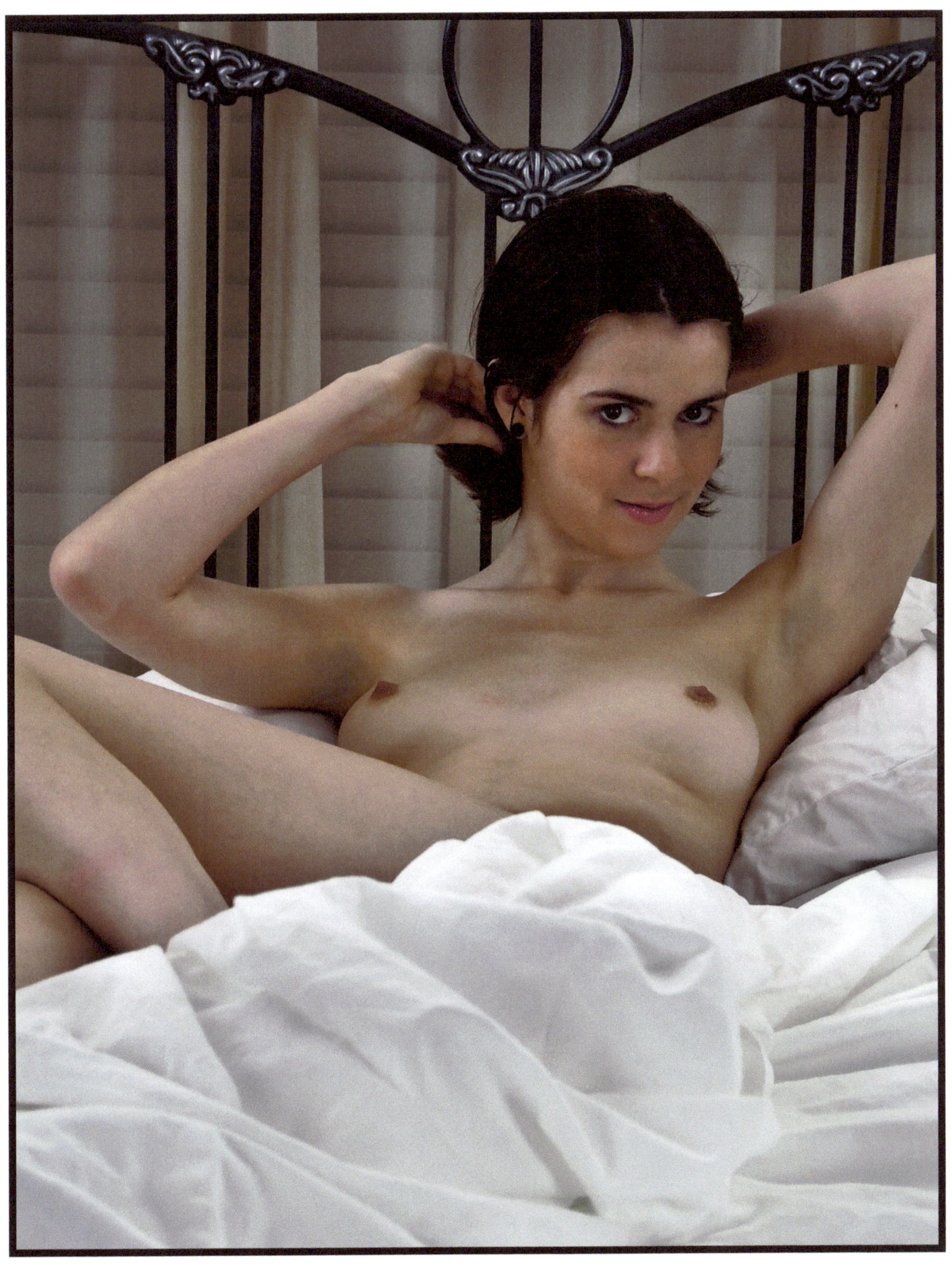

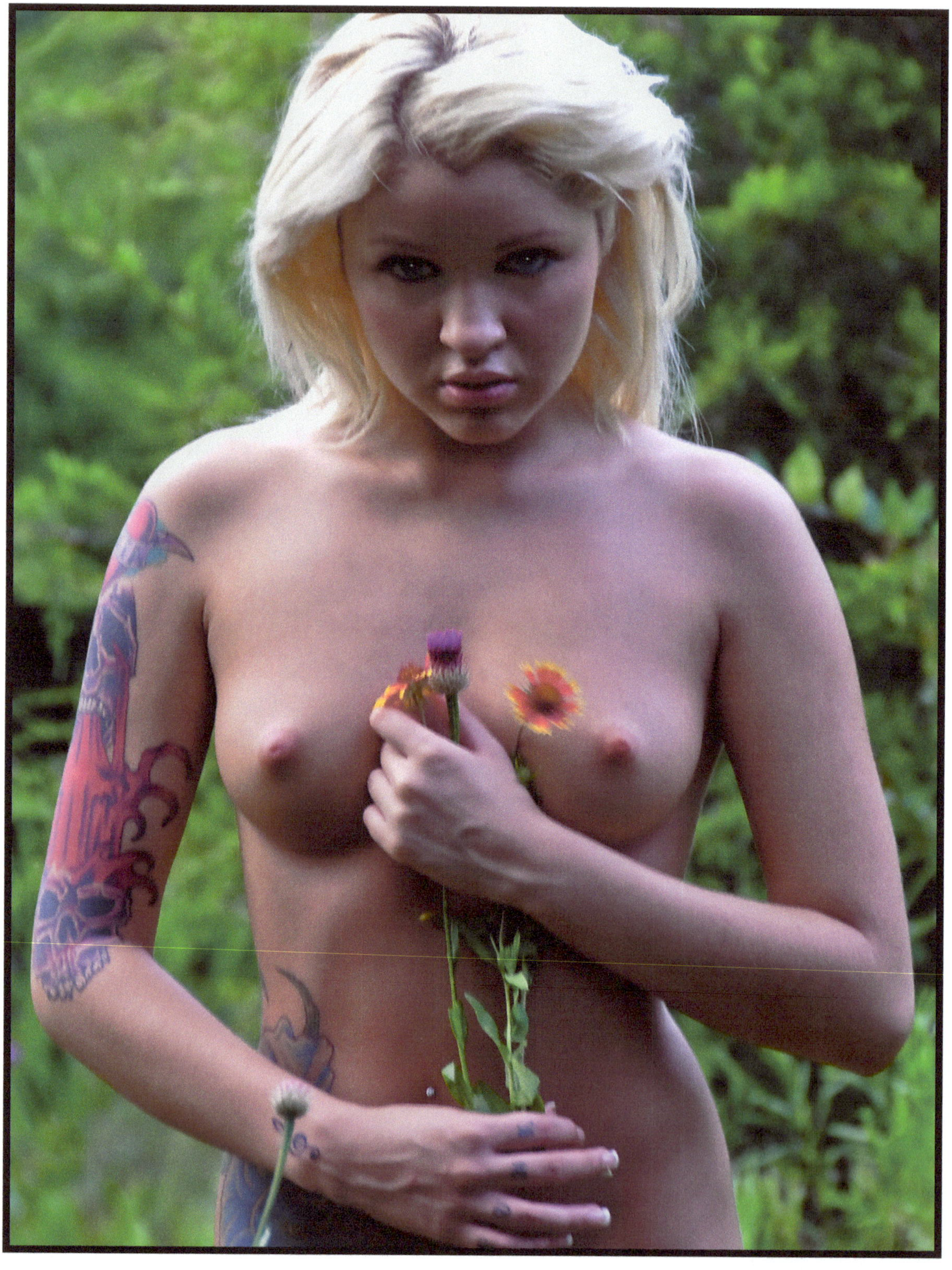

Jeska

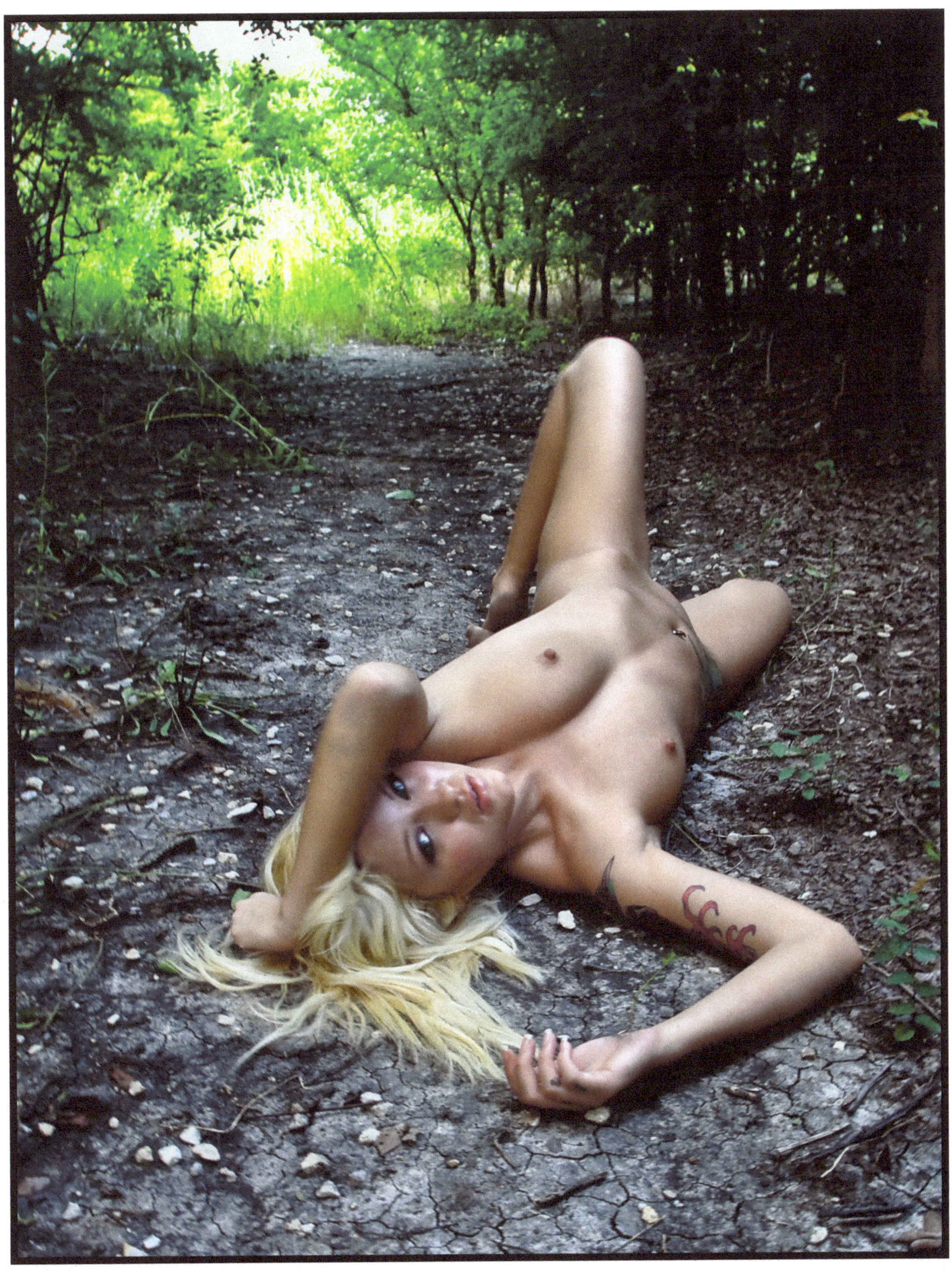

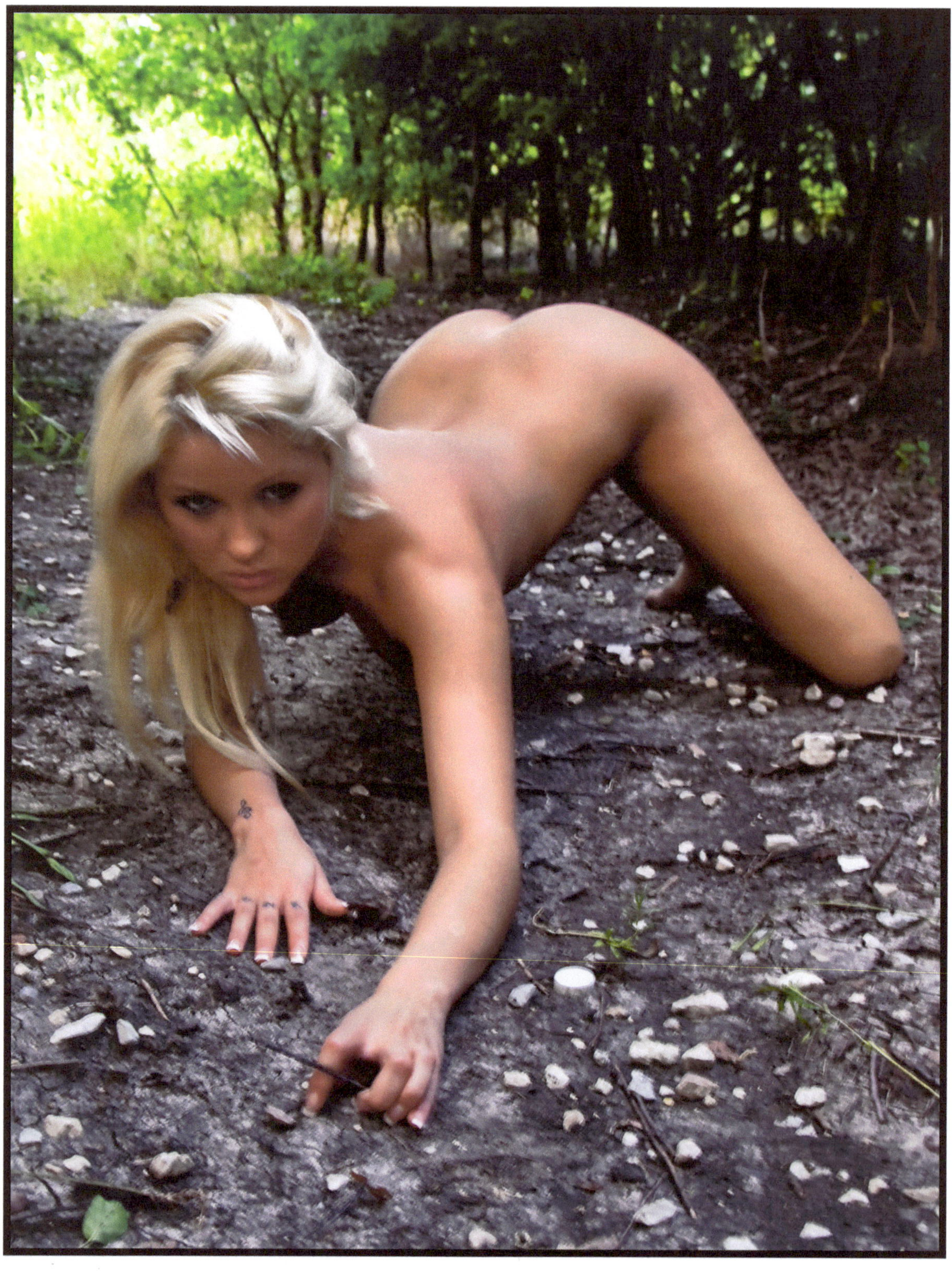

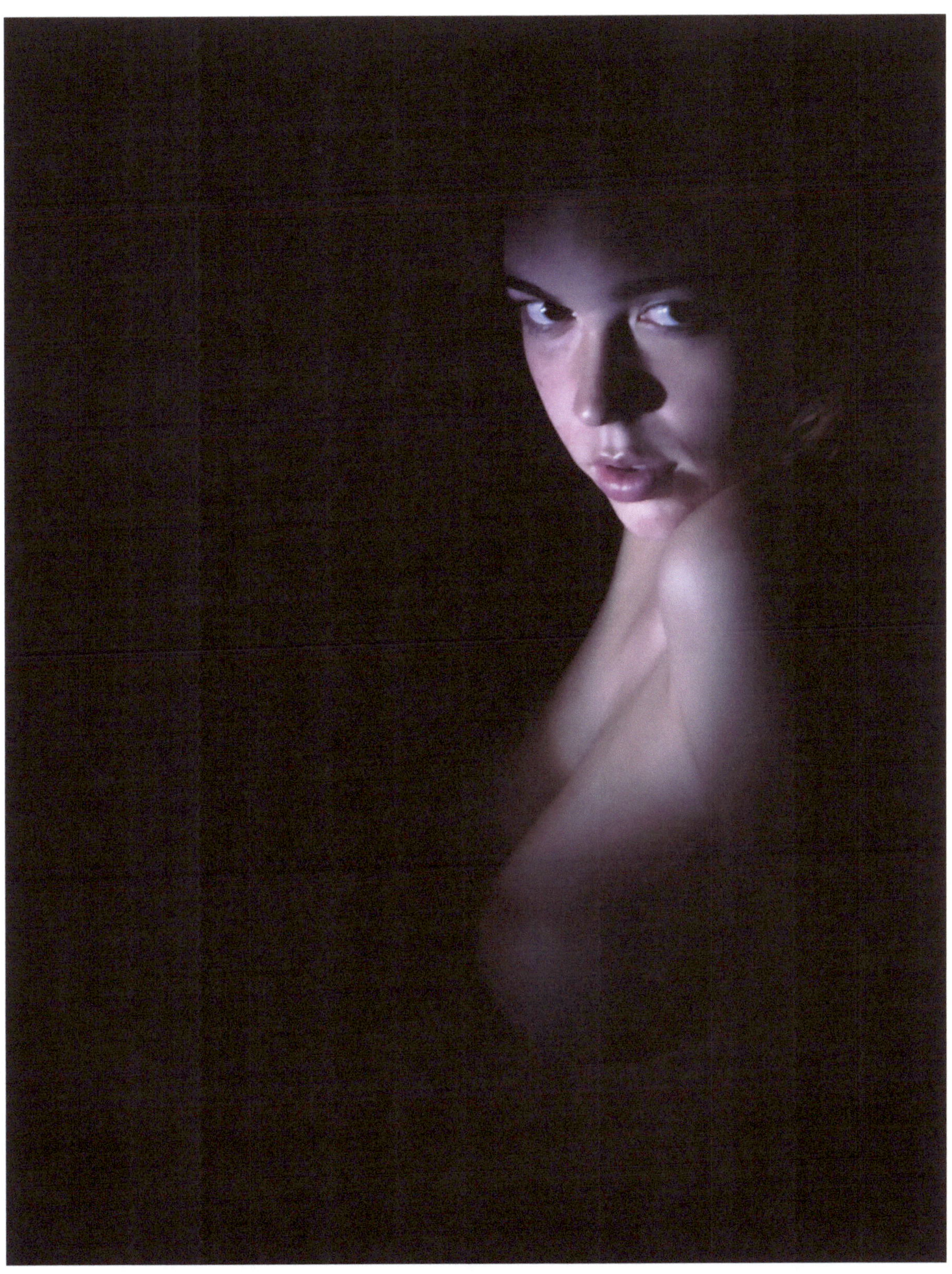

Jess

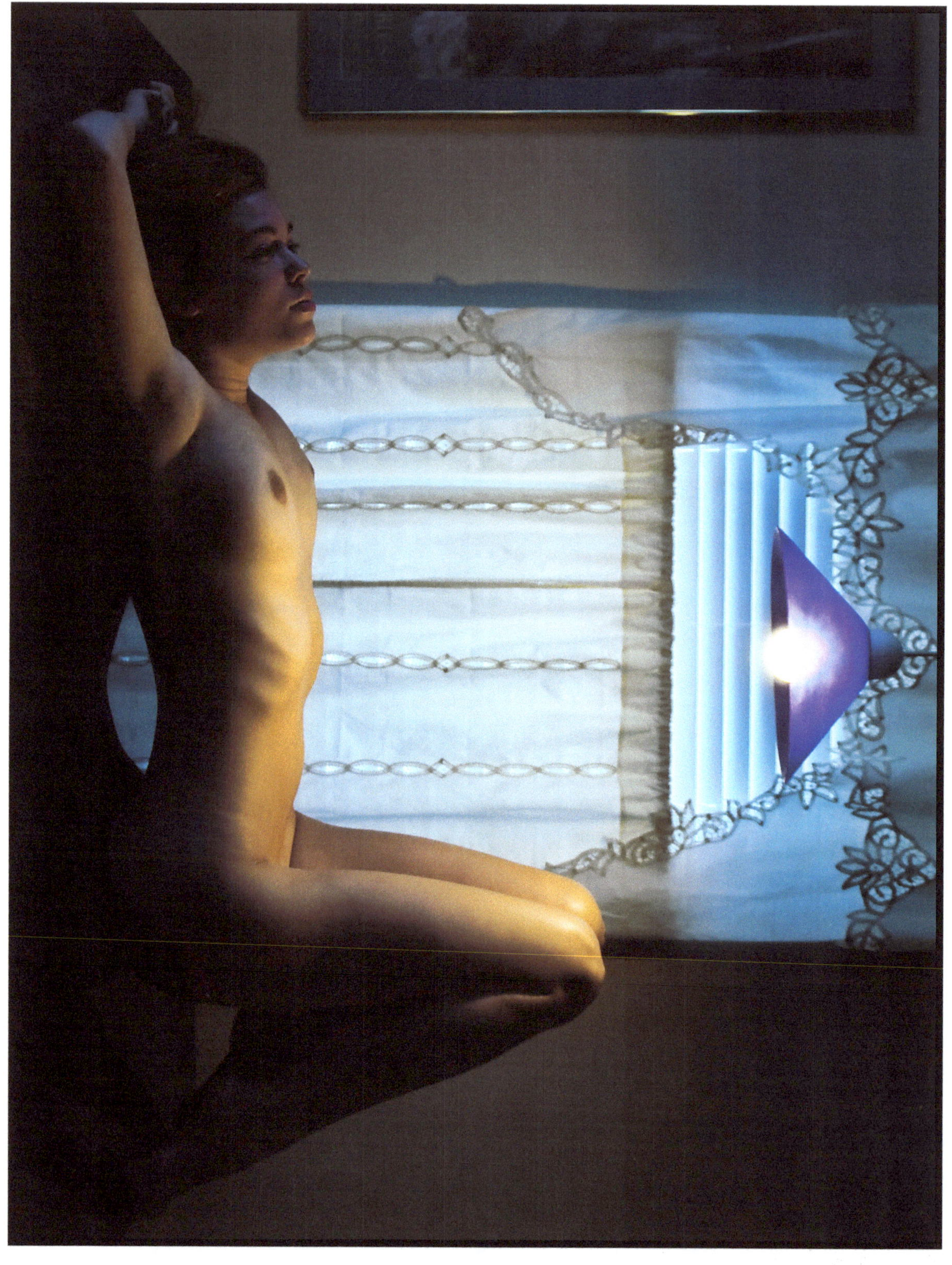

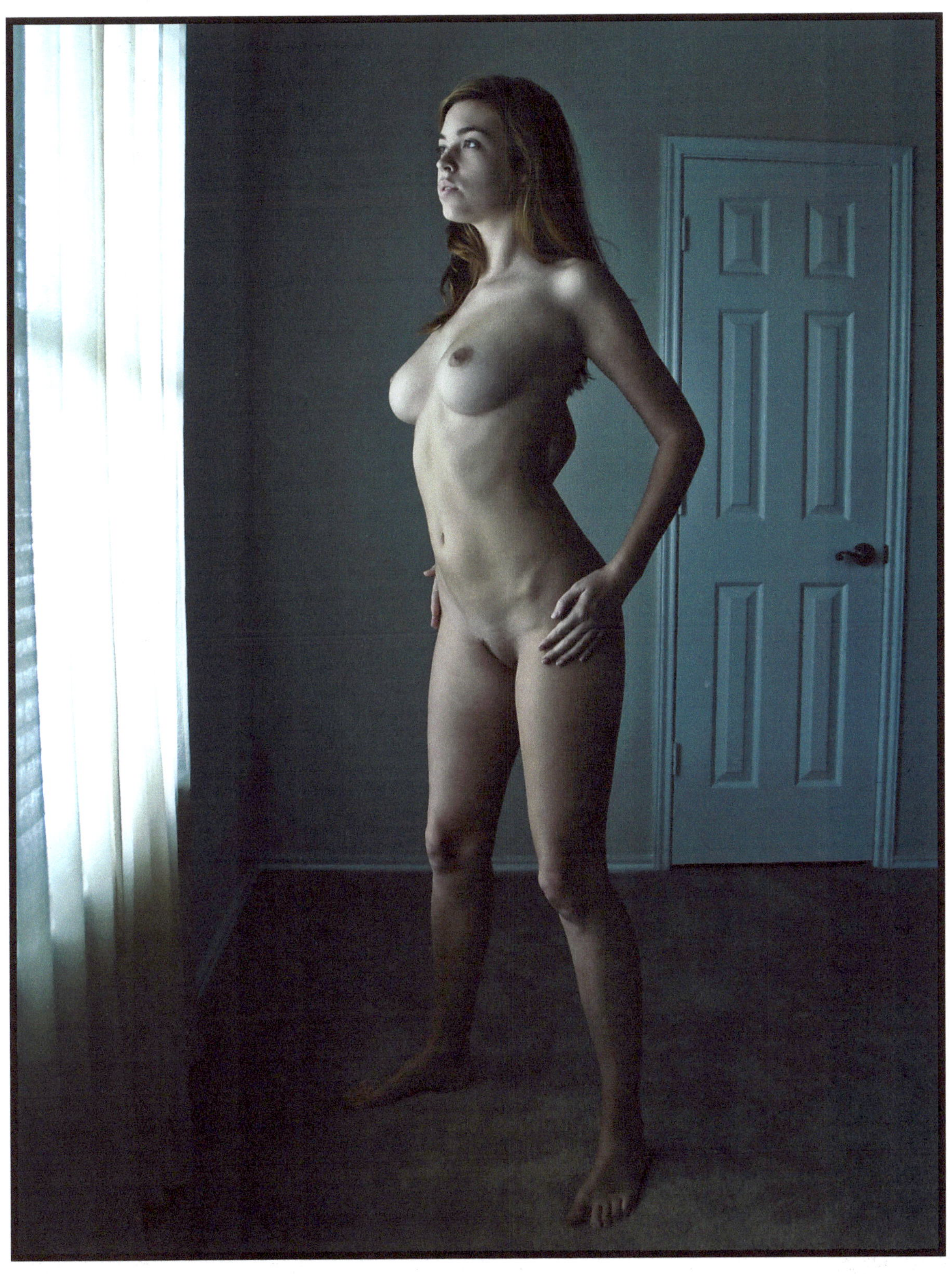

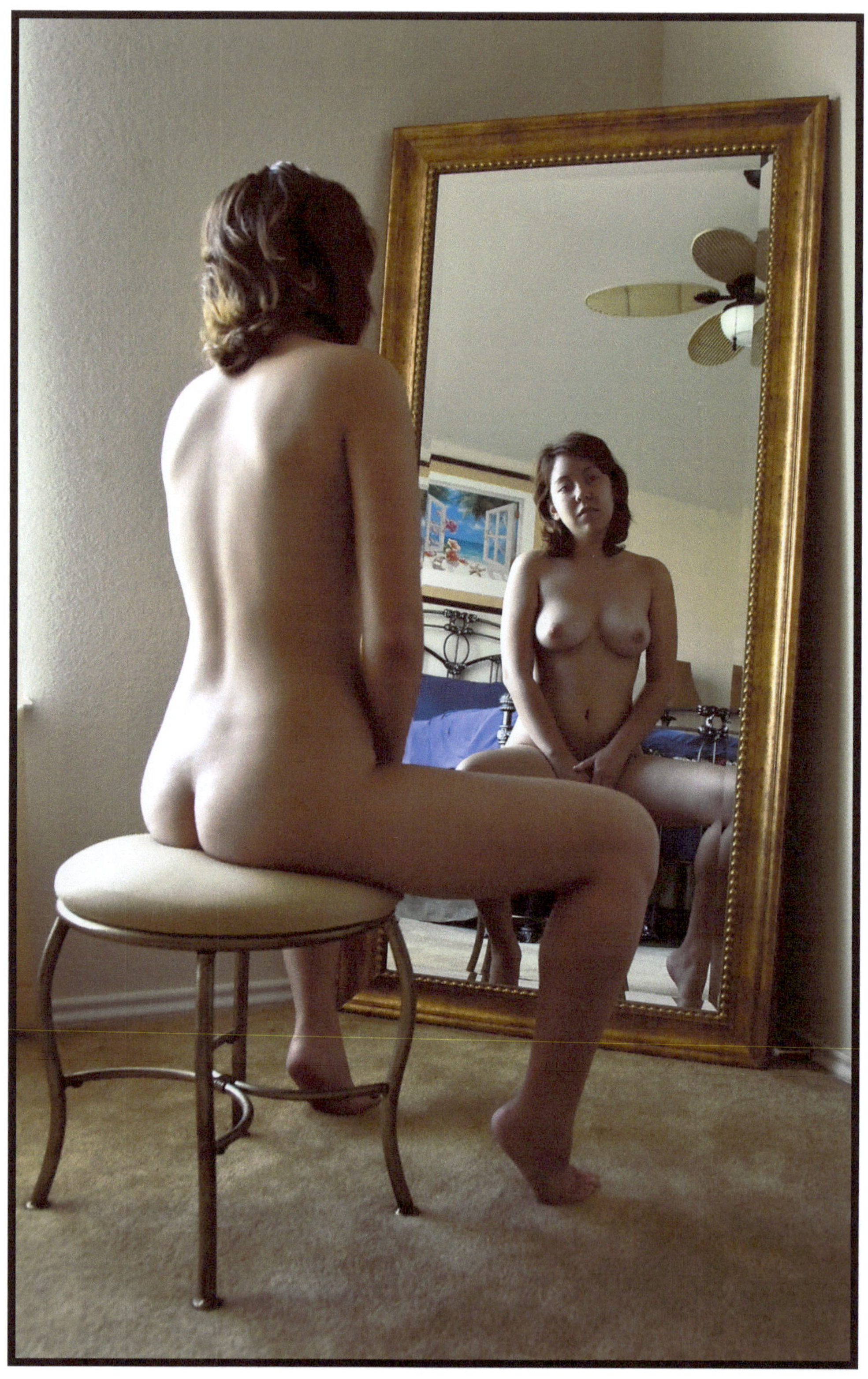

Jessica M

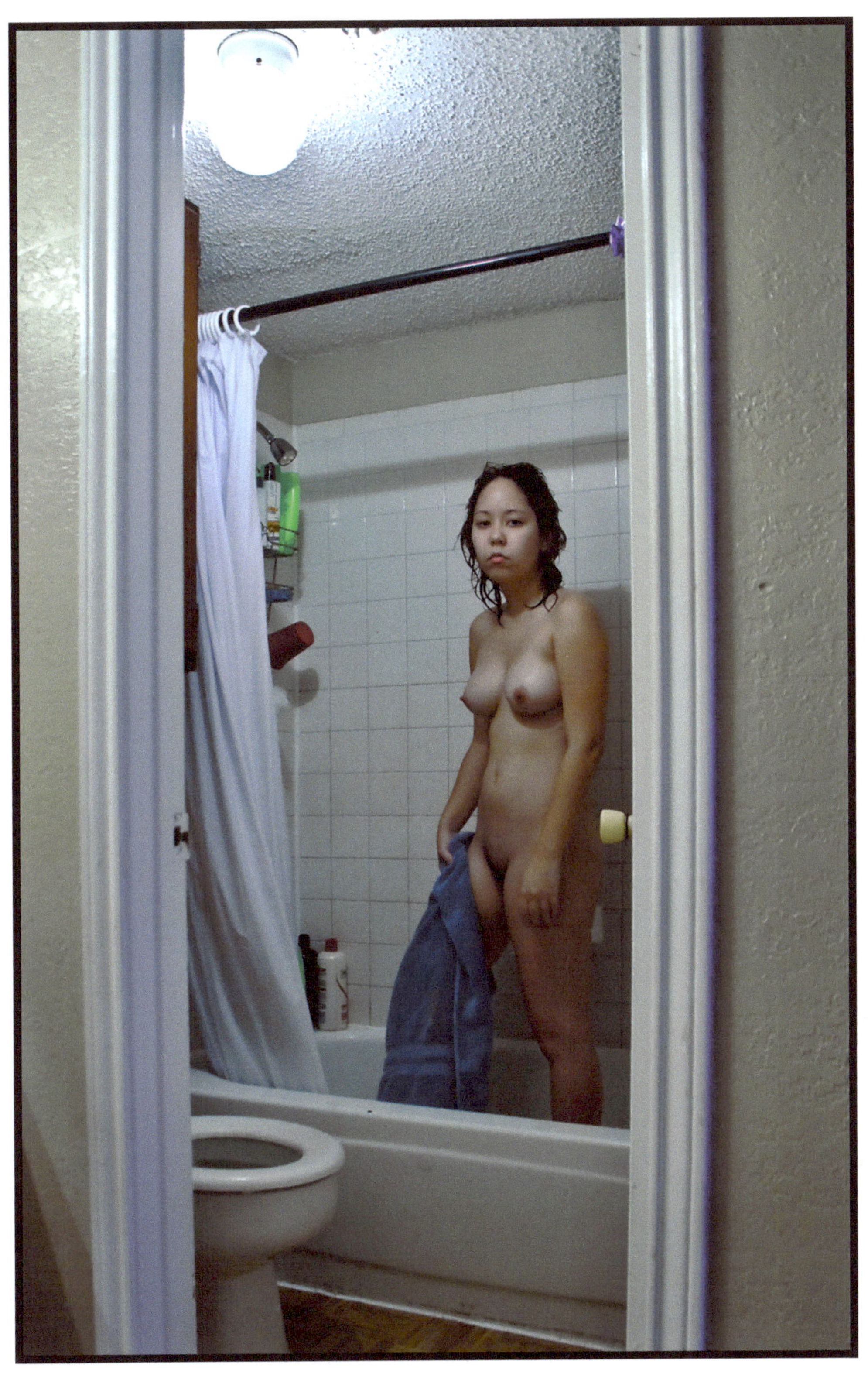

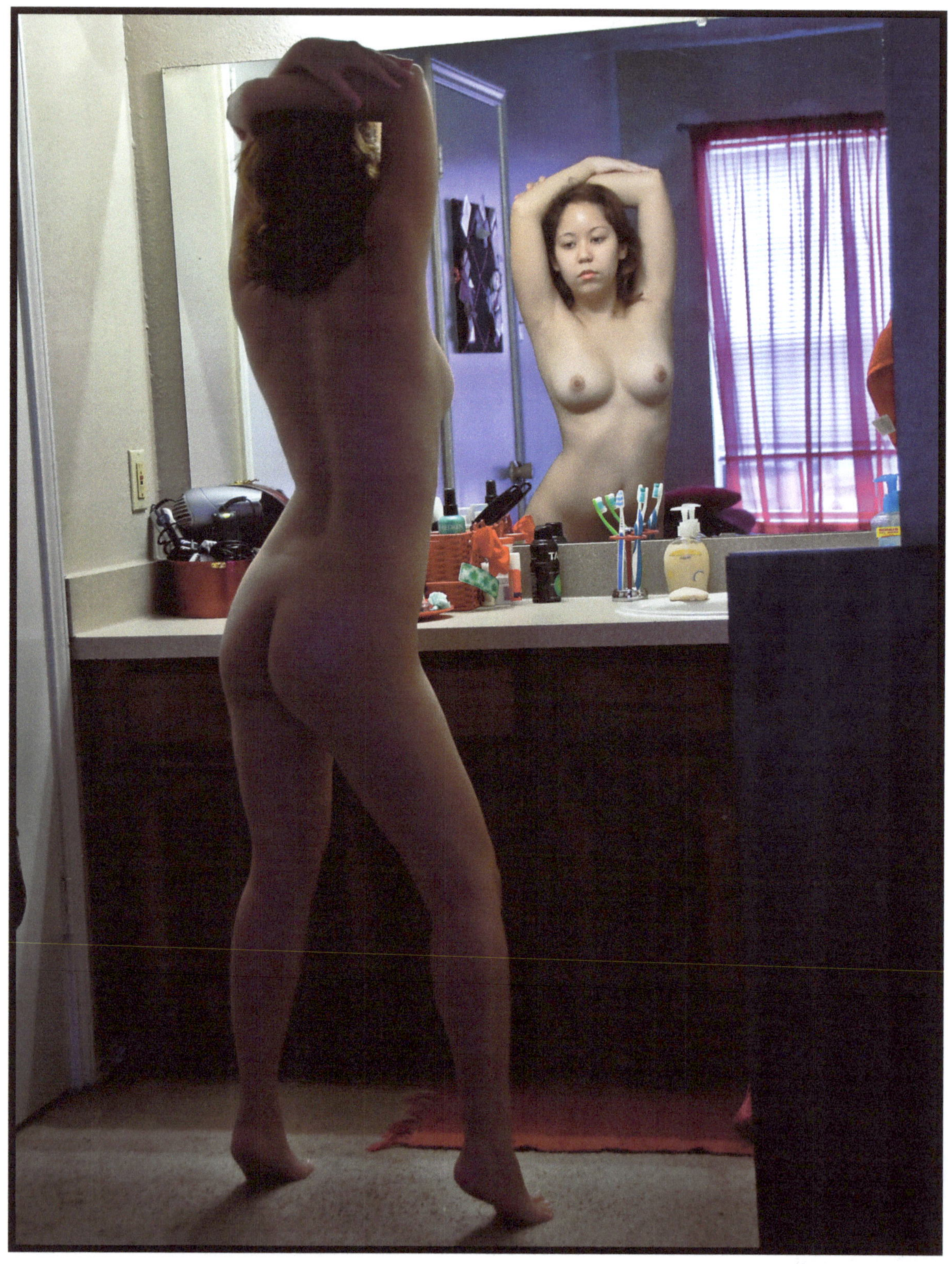

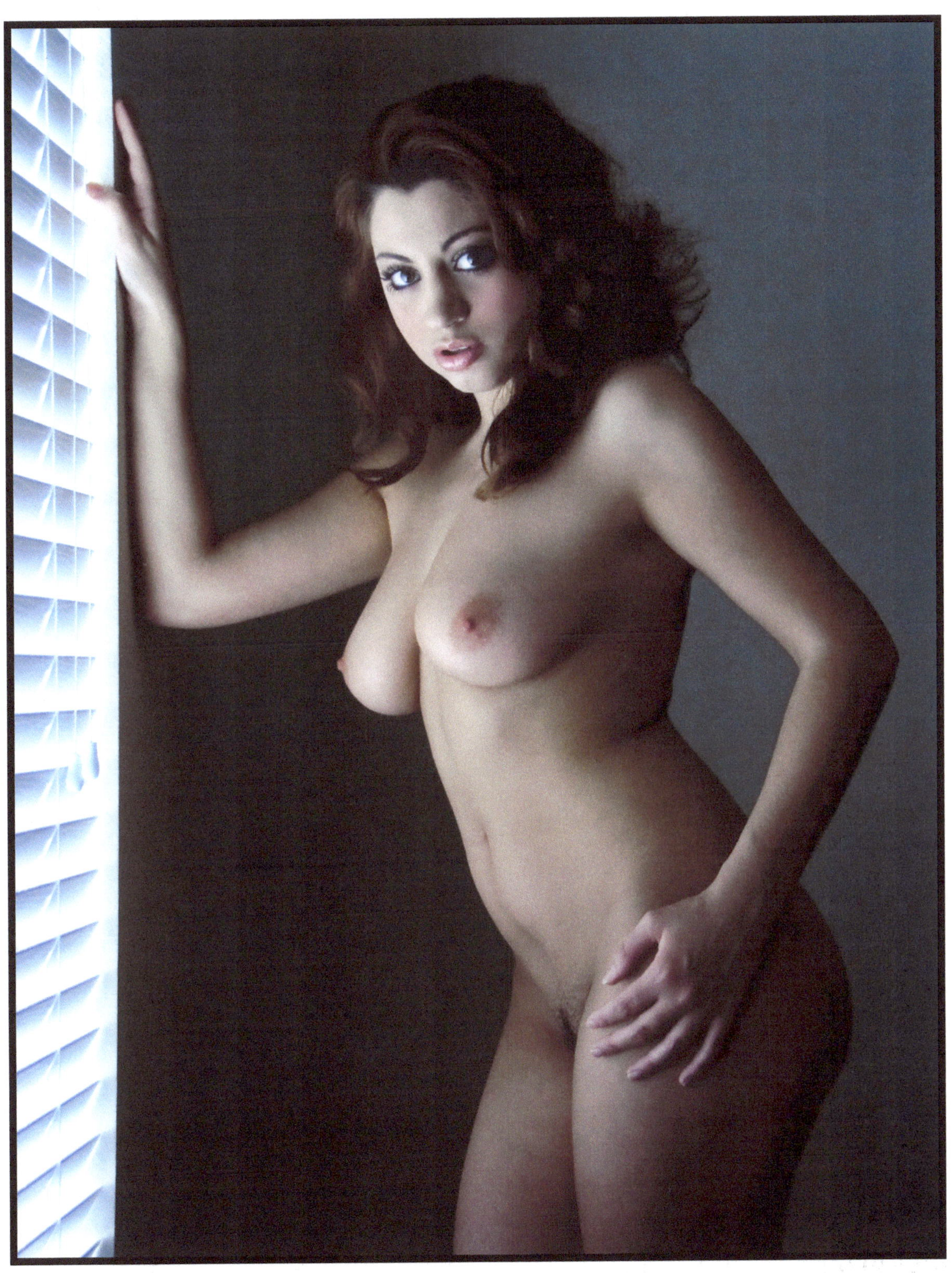

Jessica V

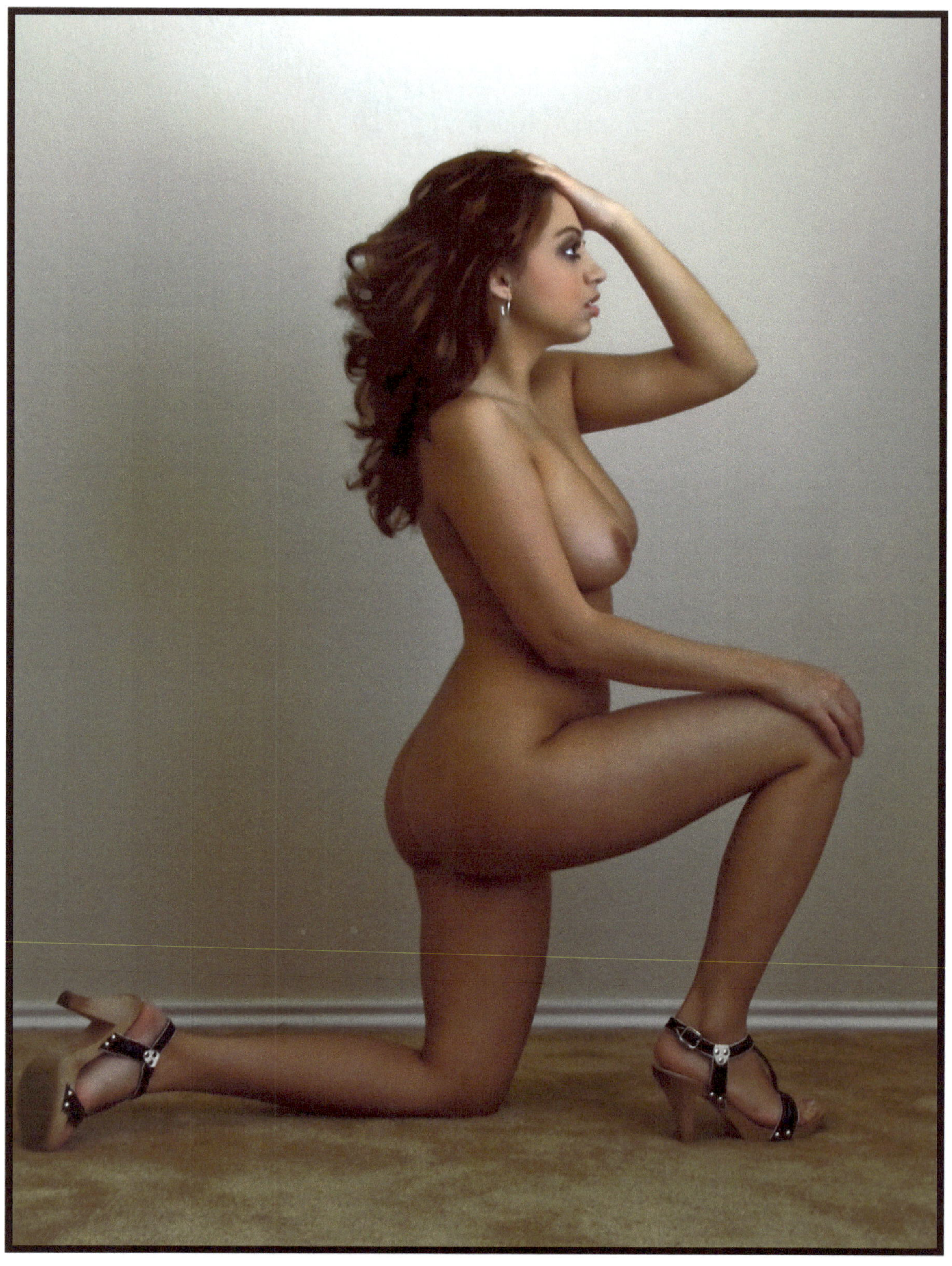

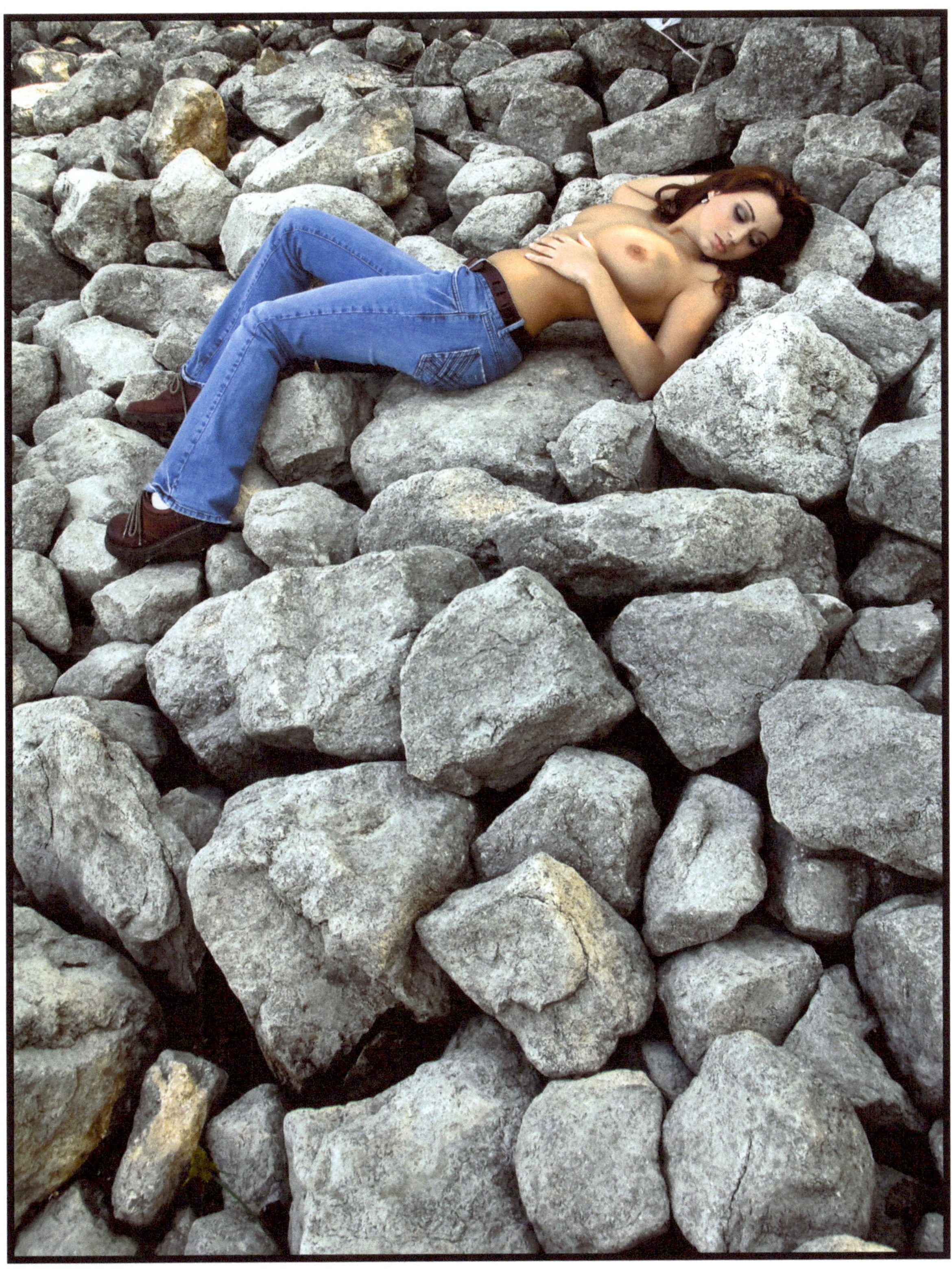

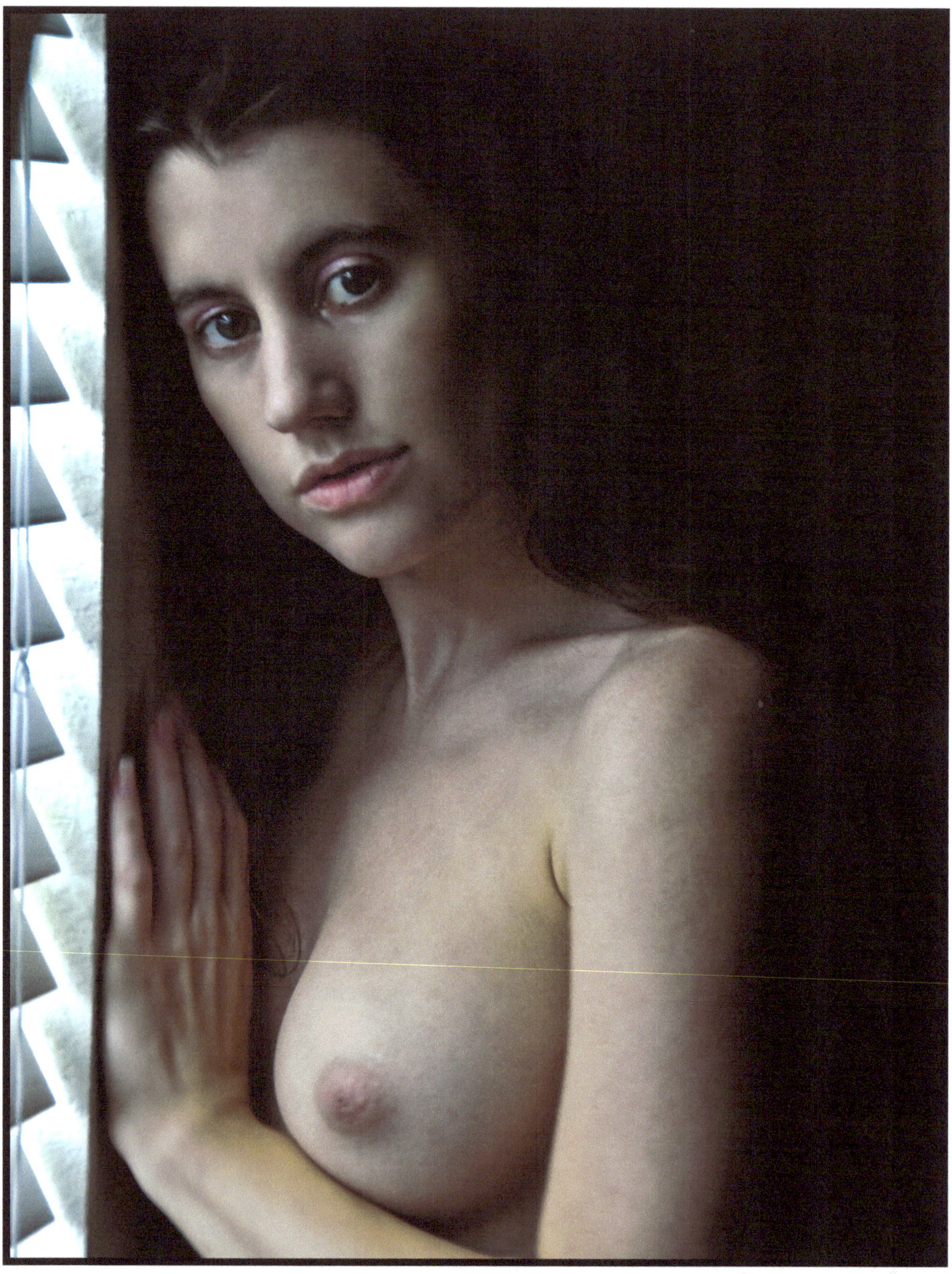

Katy

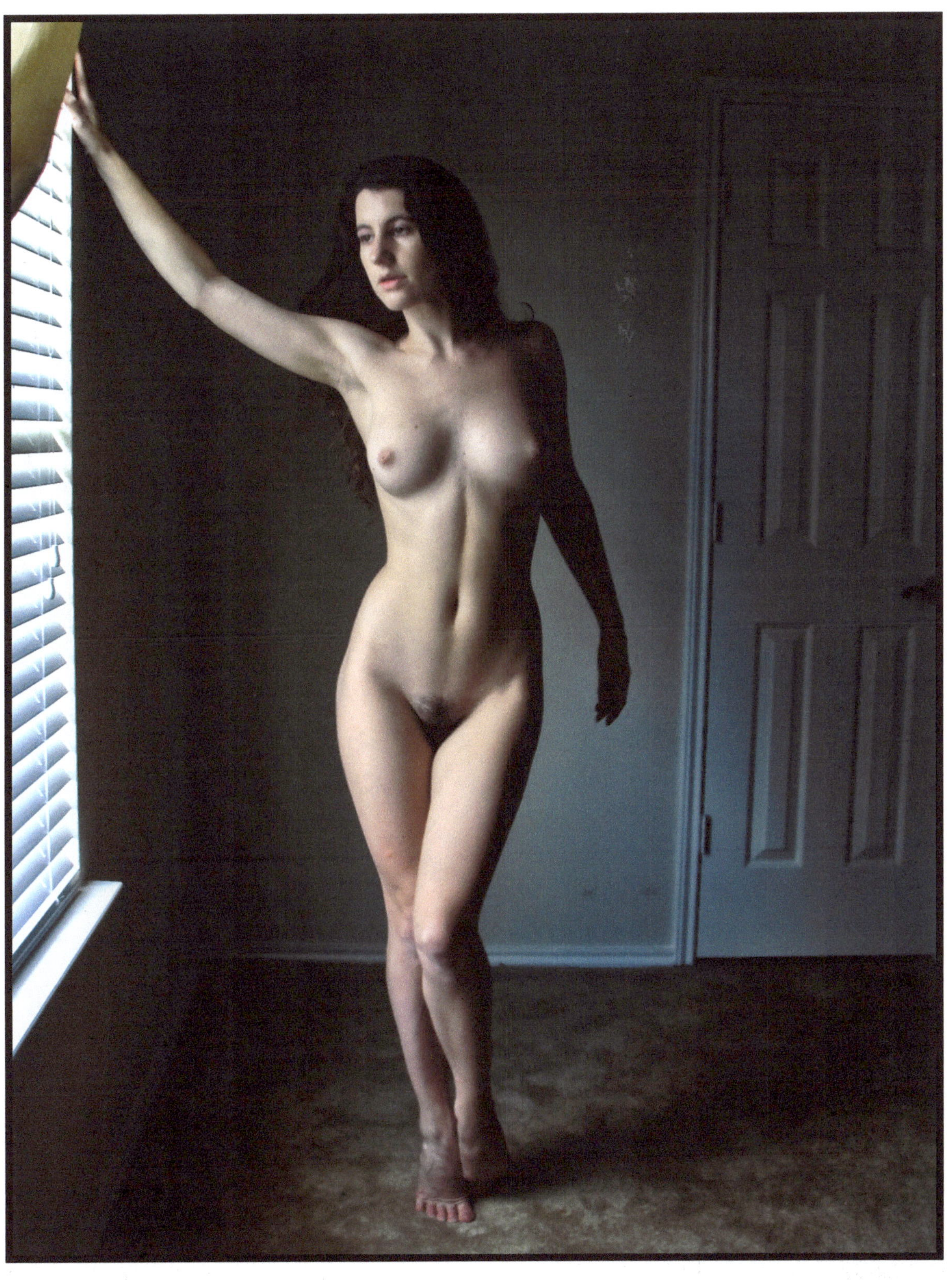

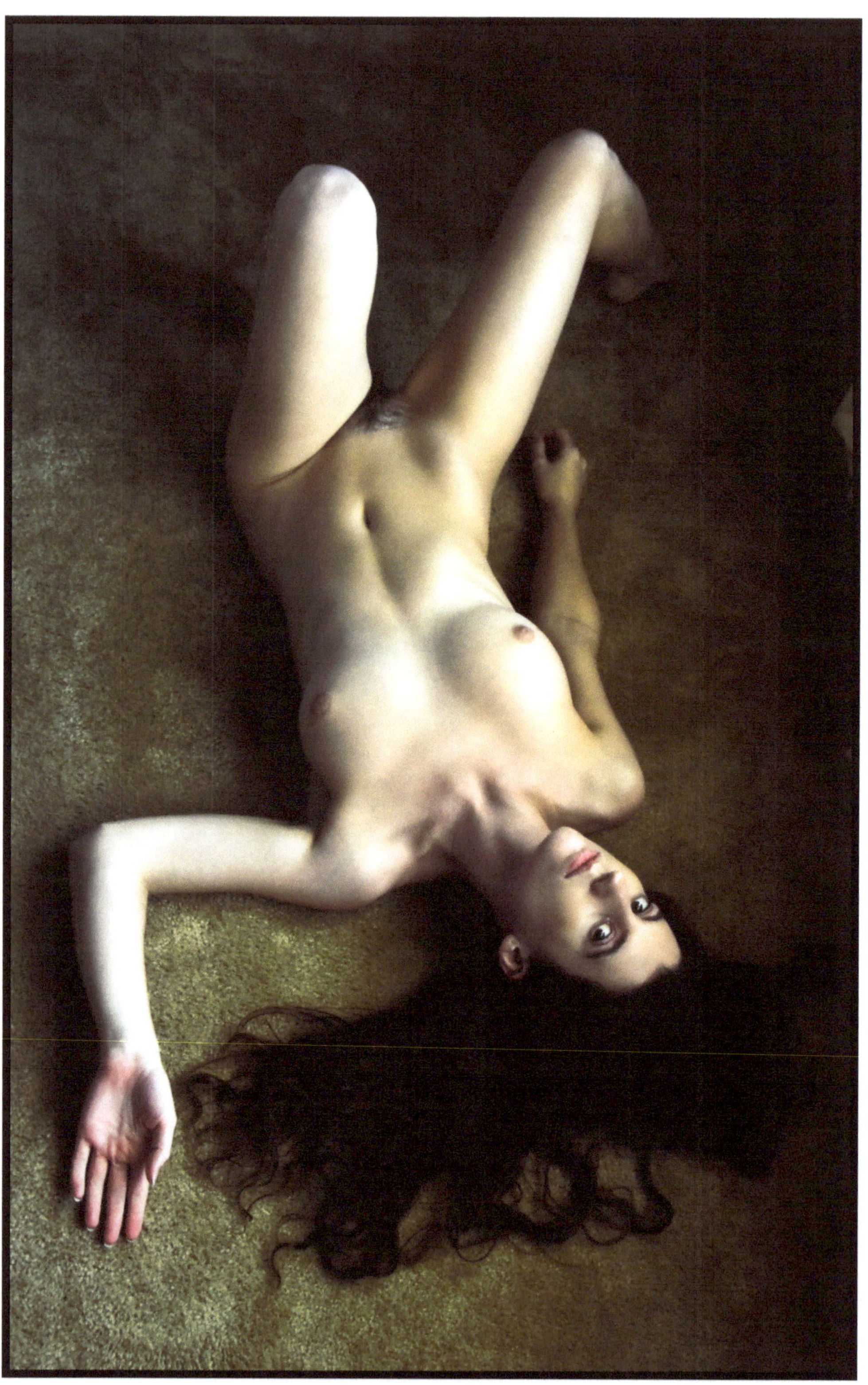

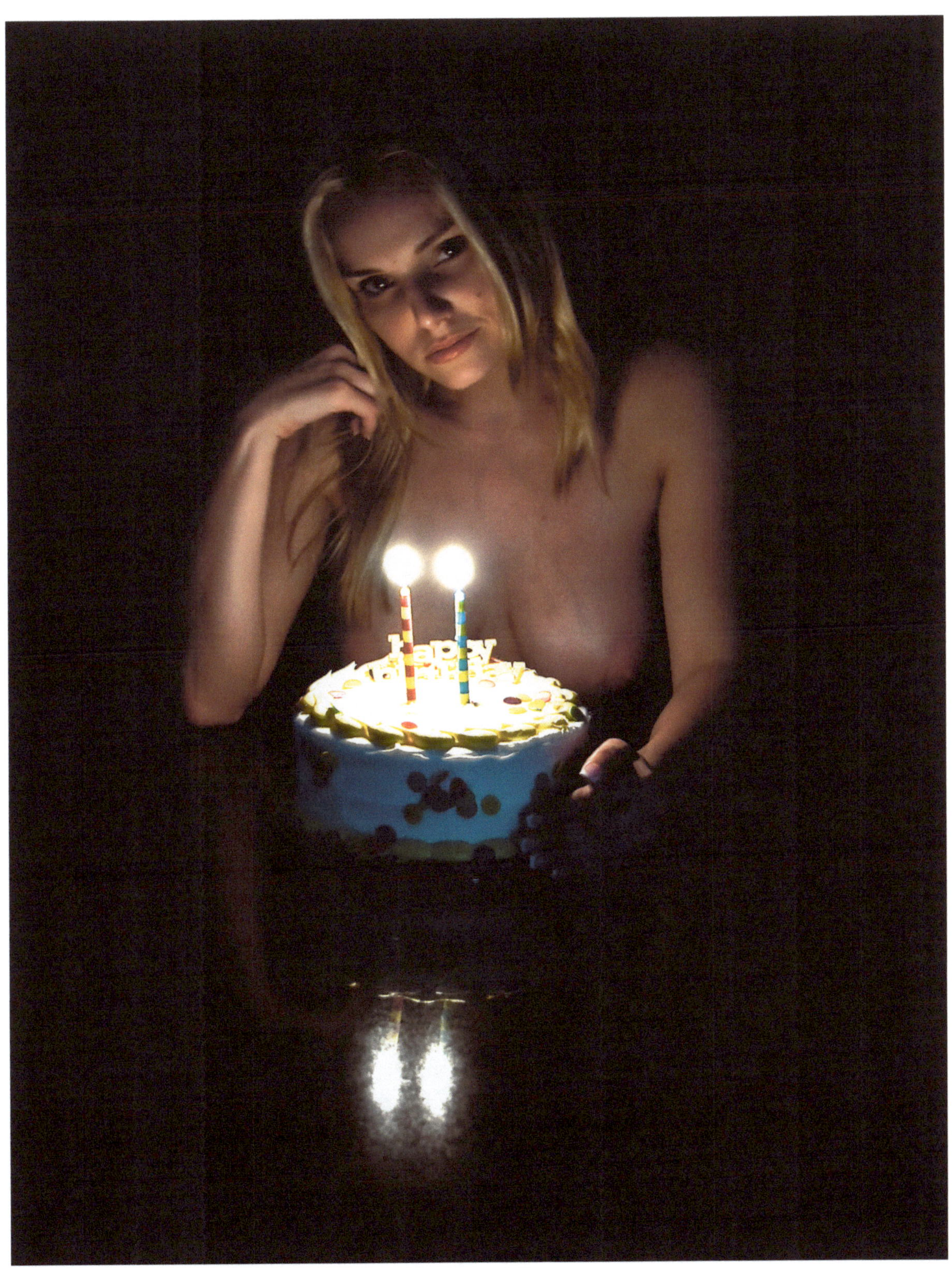

Liz

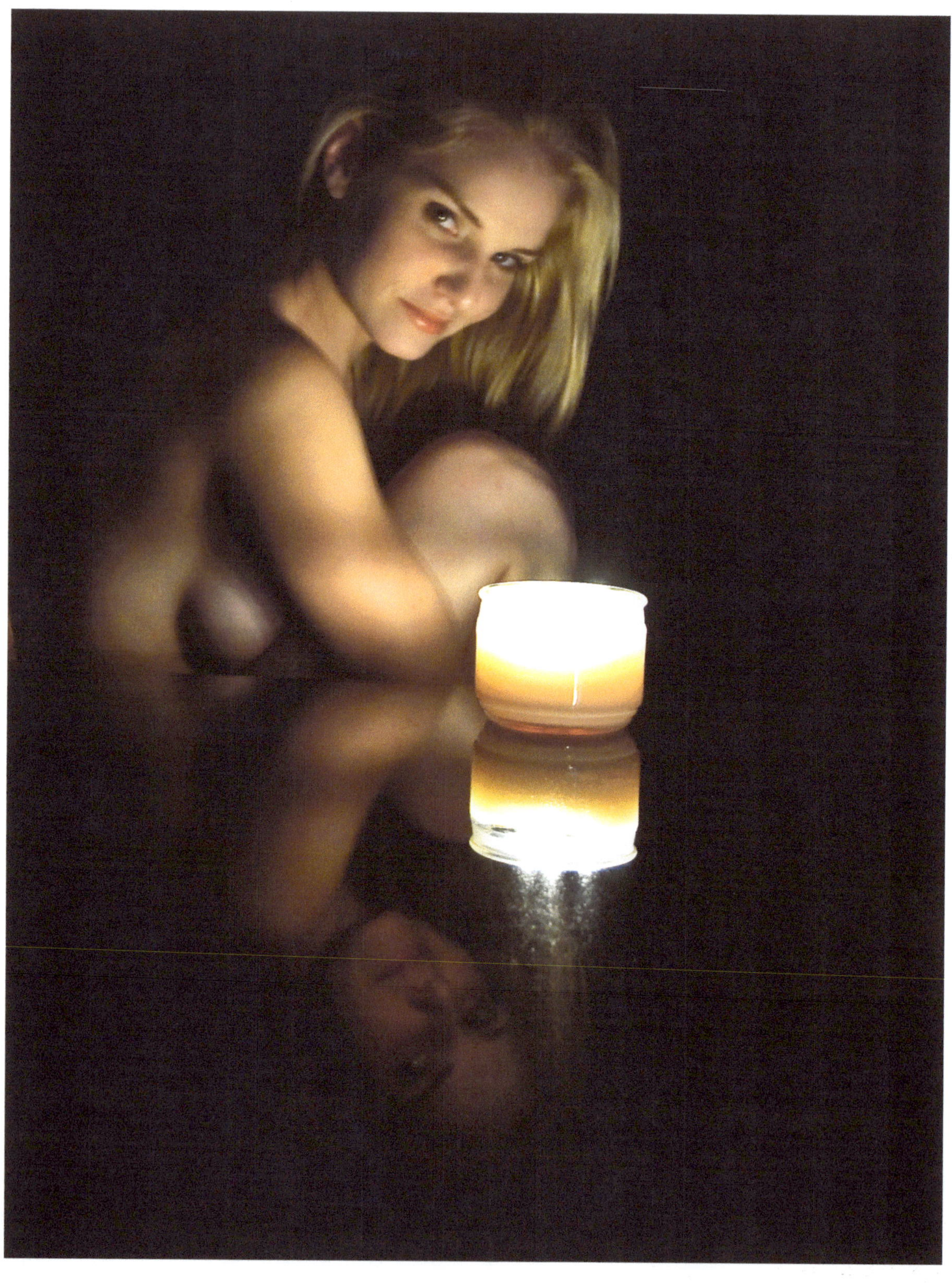

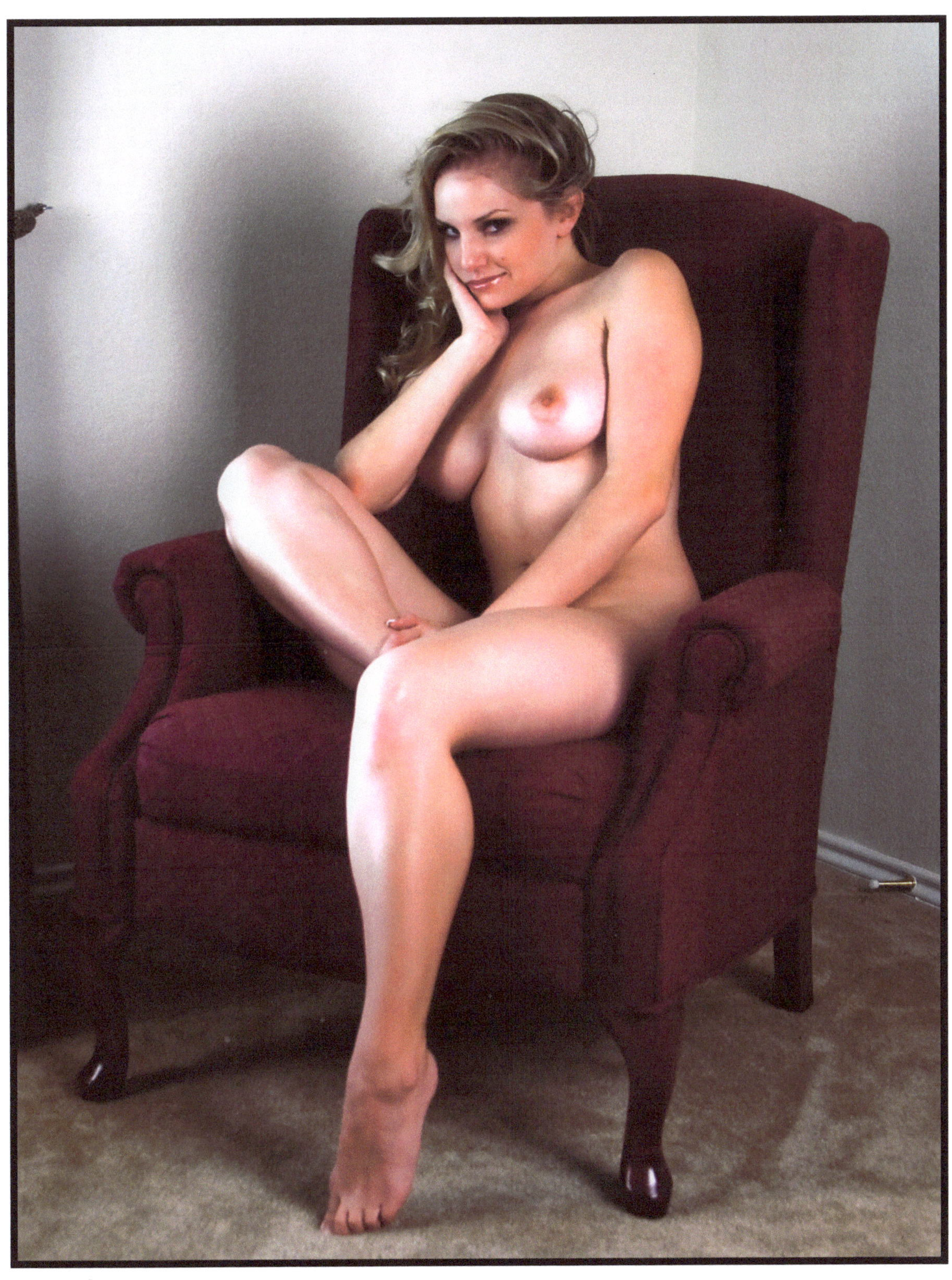

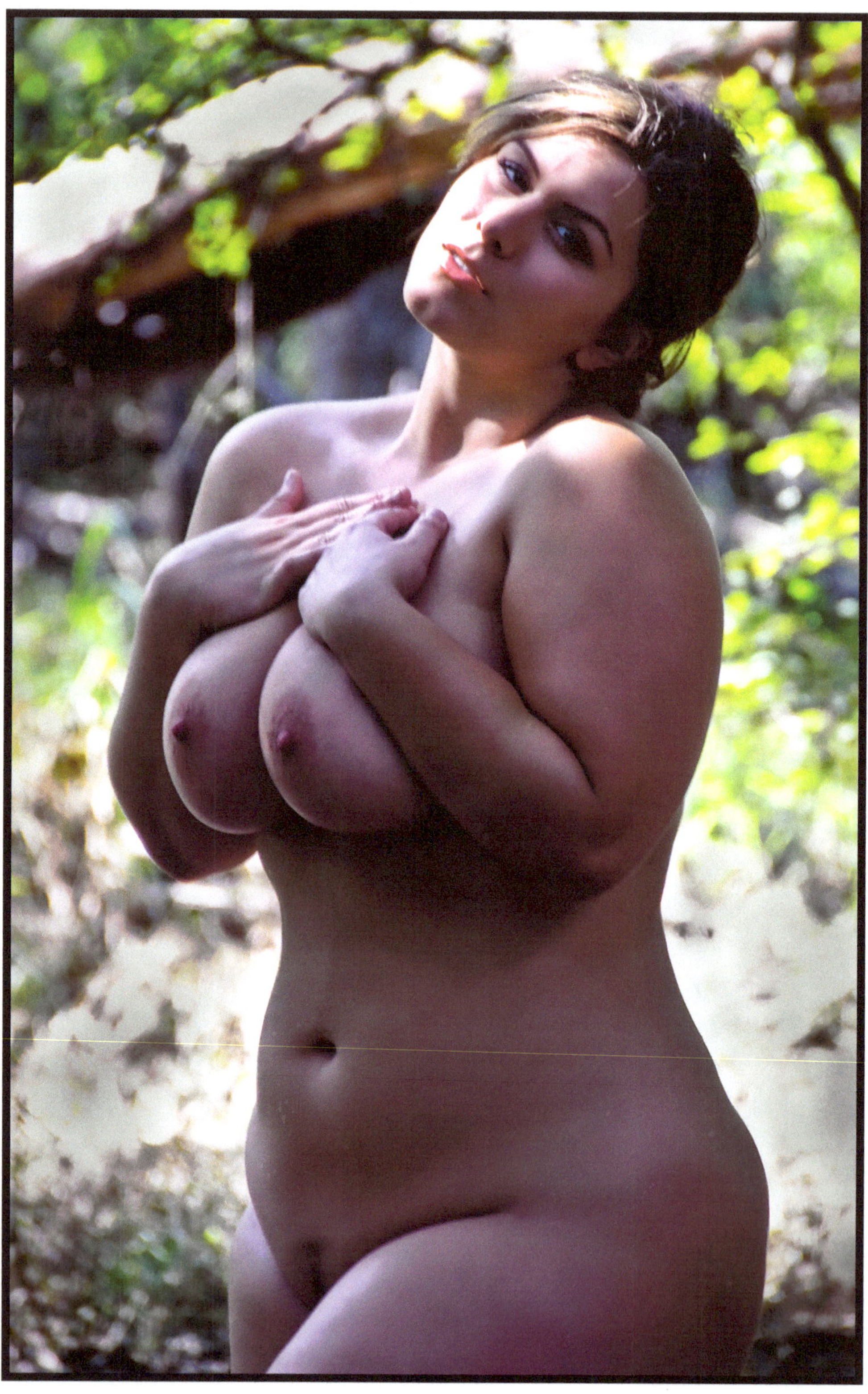

London

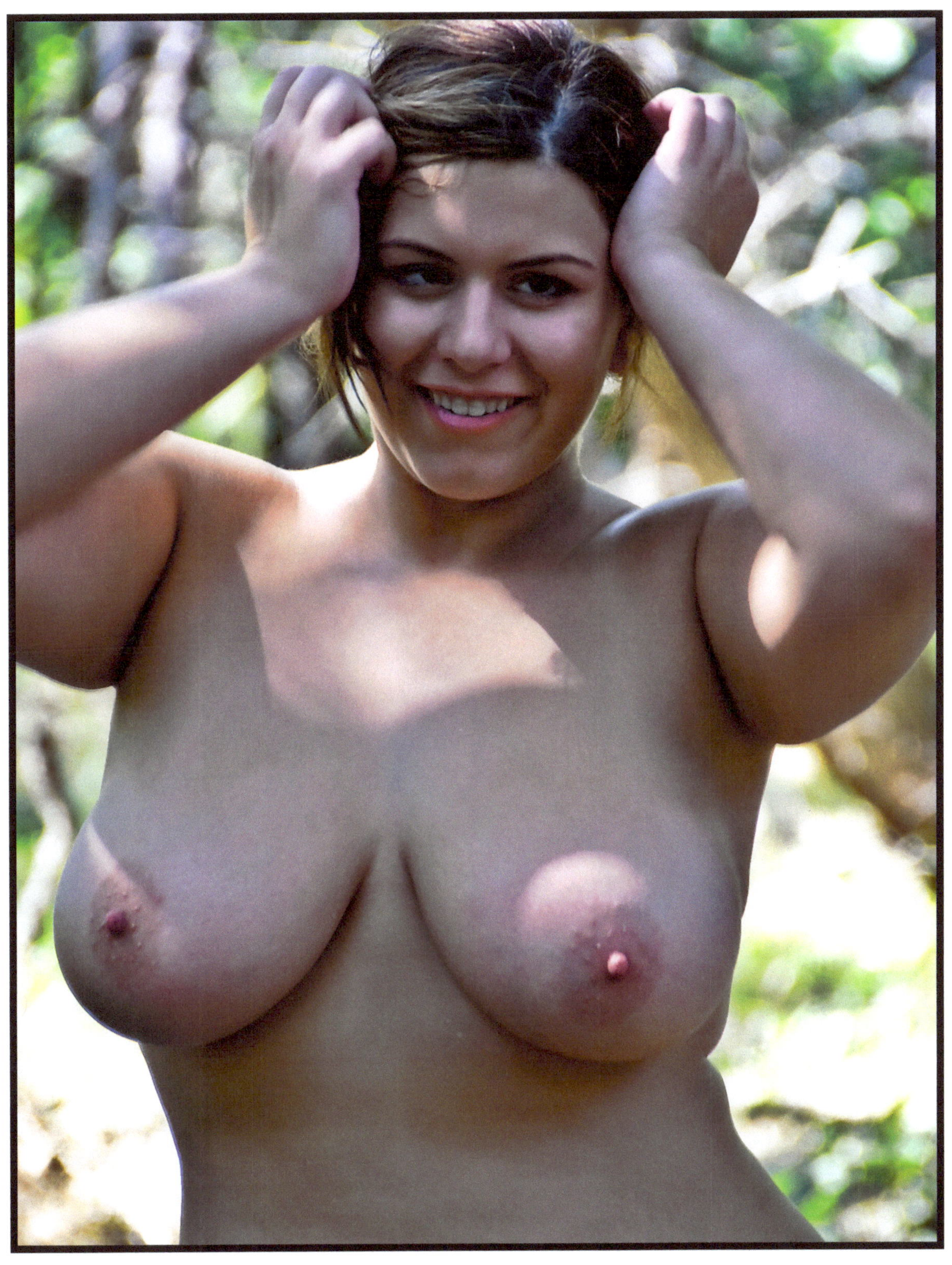

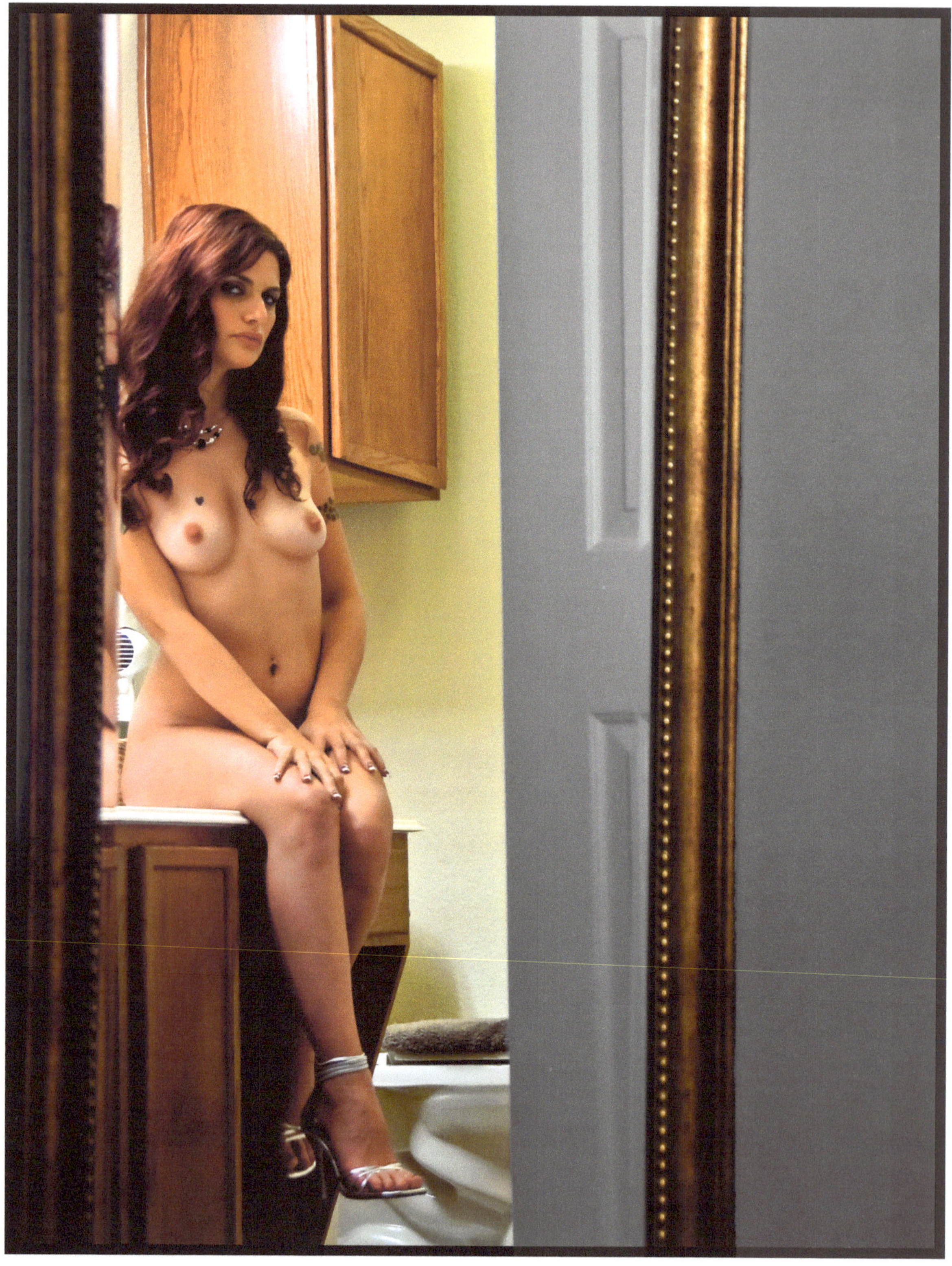

Nikki

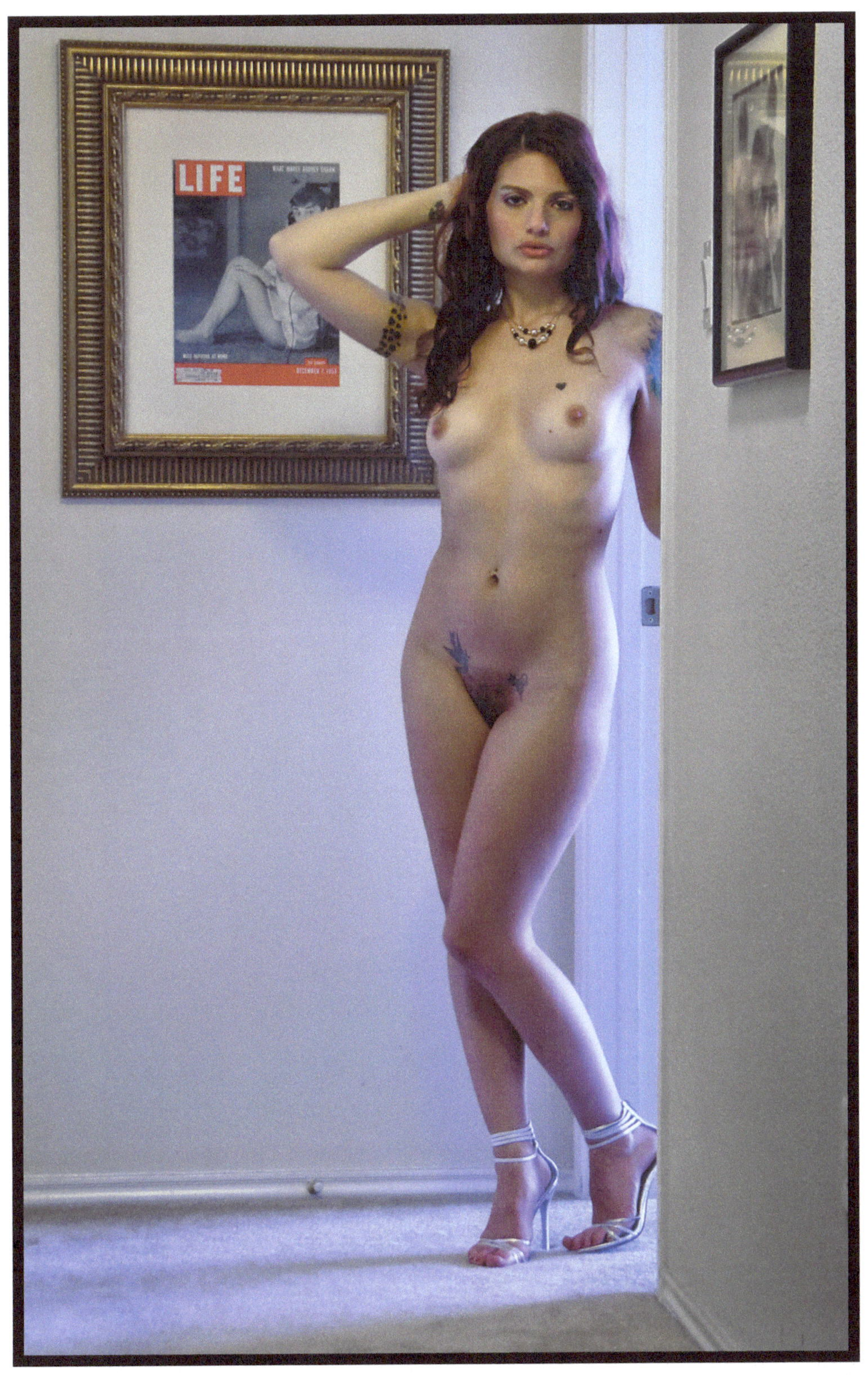
LIFE

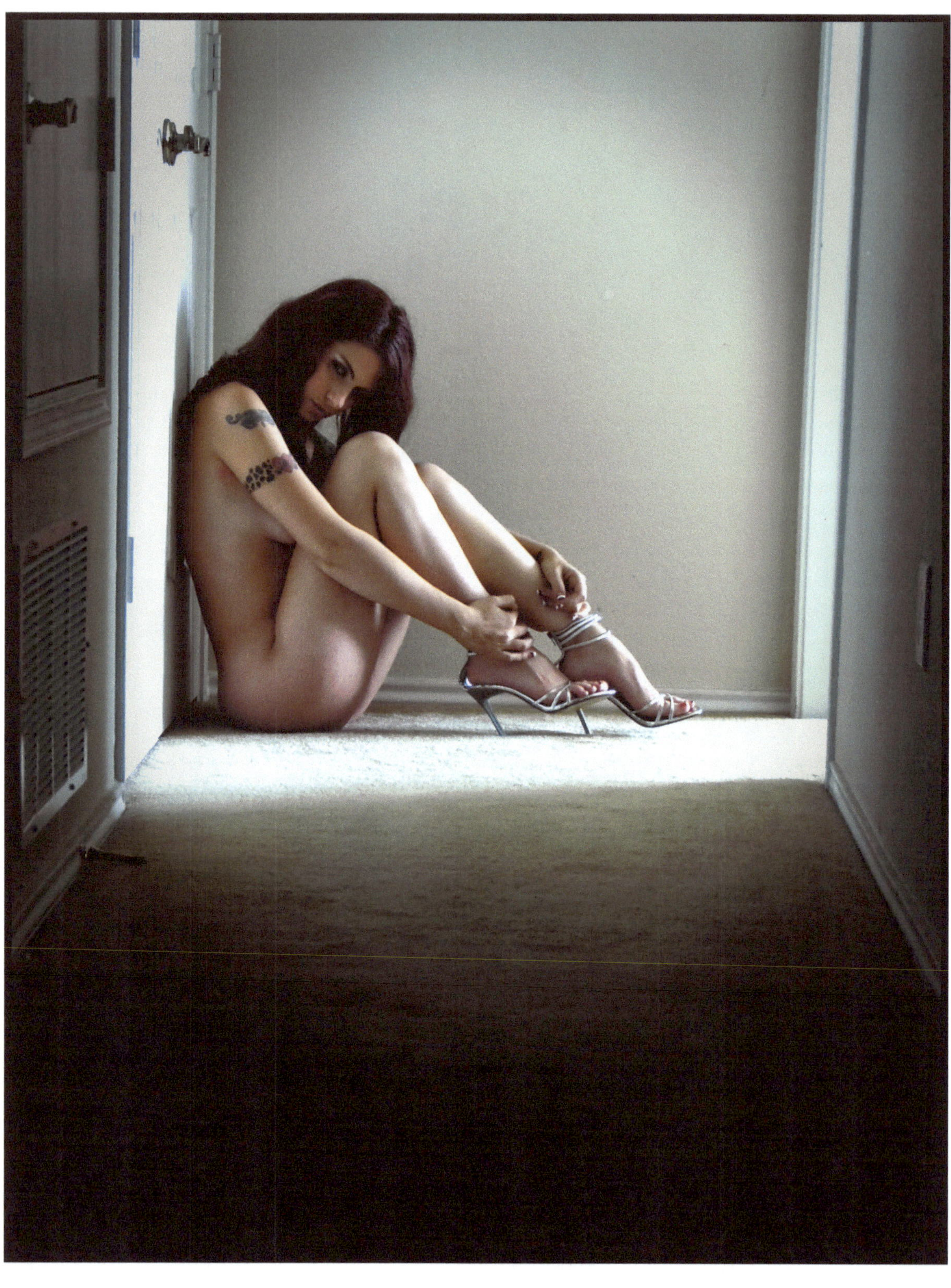

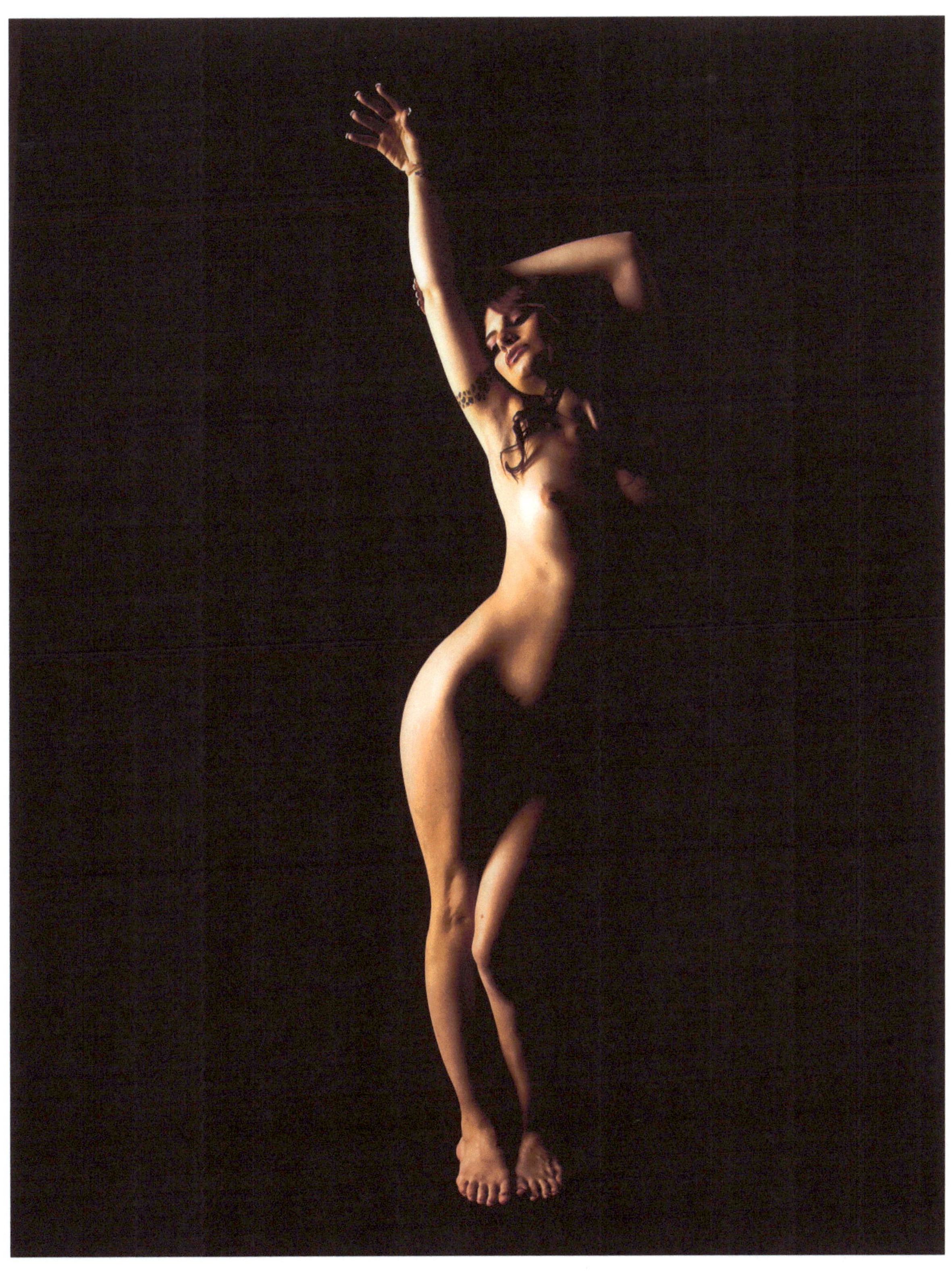

About the Author/Photographer

Born and raised in Dallas - Gary Melton is a Texan through and through. His journey into the world of photography began at the age of 20 with the purchase of a 35mm single lens reflex camera at a U.S. Army PX in Budingen, Germany. Shortly after leaving the service, what started as a hobby and grew into a passion, became an enterprise when he started a part-time portrait, team and event photography business. The magic of picture taking lost it's charm for him, though, when it became apparent that taking photos for money was a lot more about business than it was about art, so he closed the business after a couple of years.

Flash forward a couple of decades when he decided to renew his passion, but in a different direction that he felt sure would be more interesting - female figure photography. He was right, and he was also a natural at it. It took a while to make the transition from film to pro-level digital, and it also took some time learning to find the necessary artistic connections with his models - but as I think you'll see, it was worth the time and effort spent.

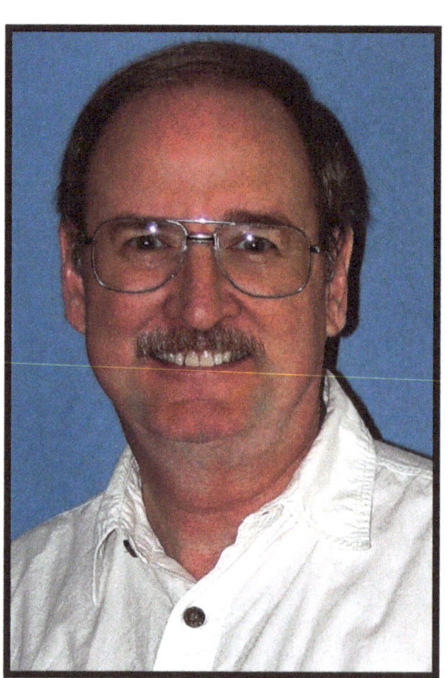

Quick Order Form

Fax Orders: 1-888-308-0462

Telephone Orders: 1-888-308-0462

Email Orders: orders@goofyrooster-publishing.com

Postal Orders: Goofy Rooster Publishing PO Box 2904 Wylie, TX 75098-2904

Please send the following books. I understand that I may return any of them for a full refund - for any reason, no questions asked.

____

____

____

Name: ______________________________________

Address: ____________________________________

City: ____________________ State: ________ Zip: ________

Telephone: __________________________________

Email address: _______________________________

Sales Tax: Please add 8.25% for products shipped to Texas addresses

Shipping/handling (US addresses only):

USPS Media Mail (2 - 8 days) Add - $5.00

USPS Priority Mail (2 days) Add - $8.50

[above rates subject to change as postal/shipping rates change]

www.ingramcontent.com/pod-product-compliance
Lightning Source LLC
LaVergne TN
LVHW070156110826
845147LV00002B/418

* 9 7 8 0 9 8 4 3 9 4 0 5 0 *